Empathy and Resilience in Education

Quick Reads for Busy Educators

Cheryl Angst

Published by Cheryl Angst, 2023.

EMPATHY AND RESILIENCE IN EDUCATION

First edition. July 23, 2023.

ISBN: 979-8223006923

Written by Cheryl Angst.

Also by Cheryl Angst

Quick Reads for Busy Educators
Gamifying Education - How to Engage and Motivate Students Through Games
Unlocking Gamification - Exploring the Impact and Importance in Education
Winning in the Classroom - Using Bartle's Gaming Styles to Empower Learners
Who Packed Your Parachute? Why Multiple Attempts on Assessments Matter
The Power of Discussion - A Guide to Using Literature Circles in the Classroom
Together We Teach - Transforming Education Through Co-Teaching
Mentorship 101 - Your Guide to Mentoring Student Teachers with Confidence
Empowering Growth - Using Proficiency Scales for Equitable and Meaningful Assessment
Empathy and Resilience in Education

I. Introduction

———

*Ἐφ' ἡμῖν τὸ μέν γε νοῦς, τὰ δὲ πράγματα ἐκ τῶν προϋπαρχόντων,
καὶ τὴν δύναμιν καθ' ἡμέραν μεταβάλλειν.*

**"The mind is the ruler of the soul, the way its thoughts go is
the way it will go."** *(Meditations, 8.48)*

———

*Ἡμῖν δὲ πρὸς ἀνθρώπους οἰκεῖον τὸ ἀλλήλοις ἐλέειν, καὶ μὴ τὰ
ἀνθρώποις ἀλλὰ τοῖς φυτοῖς καὶ τοῖς ζῴοις καὶ τοῖς θεοῖς ἐπιεικῶς
φθονεῖν· τὸ γὰρ αὐτὸ ὁ κόσμος ἡμῖν αὐτοὶ ἑαυτοὺς ἐπιτάττει.*

**"It is ours to love and have empathy for our fellow human
beings, and to show moderation, not merely toward people,
but to plants and animals. For the universe has given us
this law."** *(Meditations, 11.1)*

Importance of Classroom Community

IN THE HUSTLE AND BUSTLE of the modern educational landscape, one crucial aspect that often gets overlooked is the significance of building a strong classroom community. A classroom community is more than just a group of students sitting together in the same room. It is a dynamic and harmonious environment where students feel safe, supported, and empowered to learn and grow. In this chapter, we will explore how the principles of Stoicism can be applied to create a positive and thriving classroom community.

Understanding Stoicism

Stoicism is an ancient Greek philosophy that dates back to the early 3rd century BC. It was founded by a man named Zeno of Citium and later developed by philosophers like Seneca, Epictetus, and Marcus Aurelius. At its core, Stoicism is about mastering one's emotions, achieving inner tranquility, and focusing on what is within our control while accepting what is not.

Applying Stoicism in Education

The principles of Stoicism offer valuable insights that can be applied to various aspects of education, including the cultivation of a robust classroom community. By incorporating Stoic teachings into their teaching practices, educators can create an environment that fosters personal growth, emotional resilience, and a sense of belonging among students.

Nurturing a Safe Space

To build a strong classroom community, it is essential to nurture a safe space where students feel comfortable expressing themselves without fear of judgment. Encourage open discussions, validate their opinions, and promote a culture of respect and empathy. Applying Stoic principles, educators can lead by example, showing students how to remain calm and composed even in the face of disagreements or challenging situations.

Fostering Emotional Resilience

Stoicism emphasizes the importance of understanding that we cannot control external events, but we can control our reactions to them. Educators can help students develop emotional resilience by teaching them to focus on their responses rather than getting overwhelmed by external factors. By integrating Stoic exercises such as negative visualization and the dichotomy of control into the curriculum, educators can empower students to handle stress and setbacks with a more positive and resilient mindset.

Encouraging Growth Mindset

A growth mindset is the belief that intelligence and abilities can be developed through effort and perseverance. Stoicism aligns with this concept by encouraging individuals to focus on their actions, not their innate abilities. Educators can foster a growth mindset within the classroom community by praising effort, embracing mistakes as learning opportunities, and encouraging a spirit of continuous improvement.

Practicing Gratitude

In Stoicism, gratitude is considered a powerful tool for cultivating contentment and reducing negative emotions. Teachers can incorporate gratitude practices into their daily routines, such as beginning each class with a gratitude circle or encouraging students to keep gratitude journals. By doing so, students can develop a more positive outlook and a deeper appreciation for the learning process and each other.

Creating a strong classroom community is not only about enhancing academic performance but also about nurturing the overall well-being and personal growth of students. By incorporating Stoic principles into their teaching practices, educators can lay the foundation for a supportive and uplifting learning environment. The journey toward cultivating Stoicism in the classroom may not be without its challenges, but the rewards are well worth the effort: a community of empowered, resilient, and compassionate learners ready to take on the world.

Overview of Stoic Philosophy

BEFORE WE DELVE INTO how Stoicism can positively impact the classroom community, it's essential to gain a deeper understanding of the core tenets of Stoic philosophy. Stoicism is an ancient school of thought that has stood the test of time and offers valuable insights for modern educators seeking to create a nurturing and empowering learning environment.

The Origins of Stoicism

Stoicism traces its roots back to ancient Greece, where it was founded by Zeno of Citium around 300 BC. The philosophy took its name from the Stoa Poikile, a painted colonnade in Athens where Zeno and his followers used to meet. It gained prominence over the centuries and continued to evolve through the teachings of influential figures like Seneca, Epictetus, and Marcus Aurelius.

The Three Disciplines of Stoicism

At the core of Stoic philosophy lie three essential disciplines that practitioners strive to master:

- **Logic (Dialectic):** This discipline emphasizes the use of reason and critical thinking. It teaches individuals to question their beliefs, challenge assumptions, and arrive at rational conclusions. In the classroom setting, teachers can encourage students to engage in thoughtful debates, analyze complex issues, and hone their problem-solving skills through logical reasoning.
- **Ethics:** The ethical aspect of Stoicism revolves around developing virtues that lead to a fulfilling and virtuous life. Stoics emphasize four cardinal virtues: wisdom, courage, justice, and temperance. Educators can promote these virtues by incorporating character education and ethical discussions into the curriculum, encouraging students to act with integrity and empathy.
- **Physics:** In Stoic terminology, "physics" refers to understanding the natural order of the universe and accepting its inherent structure. It involves recognizing the dichotomy of control, where some things are within our power (e.g., our attitudes, choices, and actions), while others are not (e.g., external events and outcomes). Teaching the concept of the dichotomy of control can help students develop a more resilient and adaptive mindset, reducing stress and anxiety over things they cannot change.

Embracing the Stoic Virtues

A key component of Stoic philosophy lies in the cultivation of virtues. While the four cardinal virtues have already been mentioned, Stoics also extolled other qualities like patience, gratitude, and humility. Educators can introduce these virtues to their students and foster their development by providing role models, inspirational stories, and activities that promote virtuous behavior.

The Stoic View on Emotions

Stoicism is often associated with emotional restraint, but it does not advocate suppressing emotions entirely. Instead, Stoics believe in understanding and mastering one's emotions. By recognizing the connection between our thoughts, feelings, and actions, students can learn to manage their emotions in a healthy and constructive manner, leading to improved emotional intelligence and self-awareness.

As educators, understanding the fundamental principles of Stoic philosophy allows us to integrate these timeless teachings into the classroom environment effectively. By embracing logic, ethics, and the physics of Stoicism, we can guide students toward developing emotional resilience, virtuous character, and a deeper appreciation for the learning journey. Stoicism provides a robust framework for fostering a positive and supportive classroom community that nurtures the holistic growth of each student, preparing them to navigate life's challenges with wisdom and grace.

Stoic Values Enhance Classroom Dynamics

THE PRINCIPLES OF STOICISM offer valuable insights that can significantly enhance the dynamics of a classroom, fostering a supportive and empowering learning environment. By infusing Stoic values into the daily interactions and activities within the classroom, educators can create a positive atmosphere where students thrive academically, emotionally, and socially.

Cultivating Emotional Intelligence

Stoicism places great emphasis on understanding and managing emotions. By introducing students to Stoic practices, such as mindfulness exercises and journaling, educators can help them develop emotional intelligence. Students can learn to identify their feelings, understand their triggers, and respond thoughtfully to emotional stimuli. This heightened emotional awareness not only leads to improved self-regulation but also fosters empathy and better communication among students, creating a harmonious classroom atmosphere.

Nurturing Resilience and Growth Mindset

Incorporating Stoic values like the dichotomy of control can be transformative for students' mindsets. By emphasizing that some things are beyond their control while others lie within their power, students are encouraged to focus on their efforts, attitude, and response to challenges. This shift in perspective nurtures resilience and a growth mindset, where students see setbacks as opportunities for learning and growth rather than as insurmountable obstacles. They become more willing to take on challenges, embrace failures as part of the learning process, and persist in their endeavors.

Promoting Virtuous Behavior

Stoicism places a strong emphasis on the cultivation of virtues, such as wisdom, courage, justice, and temperance. Educators can create a values-driven classroom by integrating these virtues into the school's ethos and reinforcing them through stories, role-playing exercises, and real-life examples. Students are encouraged to act with integrity, kindness, and fairness, fostering an environment of mutual respect and trust within the classroom community.

Embracing Gratitude and Positive Psychology

Stoicism advocates for the practice of gratitude to cultivate contentment and reduce negative emotions. Educators can incorporate gratitude activities into the classroom routine, such as starting each day with a moment of reflection on things students are grateful for. By encouraging a positive outlook and appreciation for the present moment, students are more likely to approach learning with enthusiasm and engage actively in their studies.

Encouraging Collaborative Learning

Stoicism emphasizes the interconnectedness of all human beings and the importance of contributing positively to society. Educators can use this principle to promote collaborative learning and teamwork within the classroom. By fostering a sense of camaraderie and emphasizing the value of collective effort, students learn to appreciate the benefits of cooperation, diverse perspectives, and shared accomplishments.

Resolving Conflicts Constructively

In any learning environment, conflicts may arise between students. Stoicism teaches individuals to approach conflicts with calmness, reason, and empathy. By teaching conflict resolution skills and promoting open communication, educators empower students to handle disagreements respectfully and collaboratively, fostering a more peaceful and inclusive classroom environment.

Incorporating Stoic values into the classroom dynamics can have a profound impact on students' personal growth, emotional well-being, and academic success. By cultivating emotional intelligence, nurturing resilience, and promoting virtuous behavior, educators create a supportive and empowering environment where students feel valued, respected, and inspired to learn. Embracing Stoicism's teachings encourages students to approach challenges with courage, develop a growth mindset, and cultivate a positive outlook on life, laying the foundation for a classroom community that thrives academically and emotionally.

II. Understanding Stoic Principles

ἀρχὴ τῶν μακαρίων καὶ τῆς ἐλευθερίας ἐστὶν ἡ περὶ τὰ μὲν πράττεσθαι δύνασθαι ἐκλέξασθαι, τὰ δὲ μὴ πράττεσθαι ἀναμάρτητα παρέχεσθαι.

The beginning of happiness and freedom is to understand that some things are within our control and some things are not. *(Enchiridion, 1)*

Οὐχ ὅ, τι πάσχεις, καλὸν καὶ αἰσχρόν, ἀλλ' ὅ, τι ποιεῖς περὶ τούτων.

Not what happens to you, but how you react to it matters. *(Enchiridion, 1)*

Stoicism's Historical Context and Key Figures

TO FULLY GRASP THE profound impact Stoic principles can have in the modern classroom, it's essential to explore its historical context and the influential figures who shaped this ancient philosophy. Understanding the origins and development of Stoicism will provide educators with valuable insights to effectively apply its teachings in their teaching practices.

The Birth of Stoicism

Stoicism was born in Athens, Greece, around 300 BC, during a time of intellectual exploration and philosophical inquiries. Zeno of Citium, a philosopher of Phoenician descent, is considered the founder of Stoicism. He began teaching his philosophical ideas in a painted colonnade called the Stoa Poikile, which gave the school its name. Stoicism quickly gained popularity, attracting followers from various backgrounds, including the rich and powerful, as well as ordinary citizens seeking guidance for living a good life.

Early Stoic Philosophy

Zeno's teachings focused on ethics and virtue as the path to eudaimonia, a Greek term often translated as "well-being" or "flourishing." He believed that cultivating wisdom, courage, justice, and temperance would lead individuals to live in accordance with nature and achieve inner tranquility. Early Stoicism laid the foundation for the philosophy's subsequent development.

The Stoic Trio: Seneca, Epictetus, and Marcus Aurelius

While Zeno was the founder, it was the contributions of three prominent Stoic philosophers that further enriched the philosophy and its practical applications:

- **Seneca:** Seneca, a Roman statesman and playwright, brought Stoicism to the forefront of Roman society during the 1st century AD. He emphasized the importance of living virtuously and with self-control, while also recognizing the significance of practical application in daily life.
- **Epictetus:** A former slave turned philosopher, Epictetus taught Stoicism during the 1st and 2nd centuries AD. His philosophy focused on the idea of recognizing what is within our control and what is not, advocating for the mastery of one's emotions and desires as a pathway to freedom and happiness.
- **Marcus Aurelius:** As the Roman Emperor from 161 to 180 AD, Marcus Aurelius not only ruled the vast Roman Empire but also practiced Stoicism as a guiding philosophy for personal conduct. His "Meditations" provides a valuable insight into his Stoic reflections on life, duty, and self-improvement.

Stoicism's Enduring Influence

Despite the passing of centuries, Stoicism's influence has endured, and its principles continue to resonate with individuals seeking personal growth, resilience, and fulfillment. Stoic ideas have left a significant mark on various aspects of Western thought and continue to inspire individuals from all walks of life, including educators looking to create positive learning environments for their students.

Stoicism's historical context and the key figures who shaped its development provide a rich tapestry of wisdom and practical insights for modern educators. By understanding the origins and core principles of Stoicism, educators can effectively integrate these timeless teachings into their teaching practices, fostering emotional intelligence, resilience, and virtuous behavior in their students. Stoicism's enduring influence is a testament to its universal appeal and its potential to enhance the well-being and growth of both teachers and students within the classroom community.

Core Stoic Values: Wisdom, Courage, Justice, Temperance

AT THE HEART OF STOICISM lies a set of core values that form the foundation for living a virtuous and fulfilling life. These values, known as the four cardinal virtues, encompass qualities that Stoics believe are essential for achieving inner tranquility and leading a life of purpose. As educators seek to incorporate Stoic principles into their classrooms, understanding and promoting these core values becomes paramount in creating a positive and growth-oriented learning environment.

Wisdom (Sophia)

Wisdom is the cornerstone of Stoic philosophy and serves as a guiding light for decision-making and understanding the world. In the context of Stoicism, wisdom goes beyond mere academic knowledge; it entails the ability to discern what is truly important and valuable in life. For educators, fostering wisdom means encouraging students to think critically, analyze information, and seek deeper insights. Engaging in thoughtful discussions, exploring diverse perspectives, and encouraging intellectual curiosity can nurture the development of wisdom within the classroom.

Courage (Andreia)

Courage is the virtue that empowers individuals to face adversity, challenges, and fears with inner strength and resilience. Stoics view courage not as an absence of fear, but as the ability to act in the face of fear while staying true to one's values. Educators can cultivate courage in students by creating a safe space where risk-taking is encouraged, mistakes are seen as opportunities for growth, and students are supported in their pursuit of their goals. By praising acts of bravery, whether big or small, educators inspire students to develop the courage to tackle challenges and embrace new experiences.

Justice (Dikaiosyne)

Justice in Stoicism is not limited to the administration of laws or fairness in a legal sense but extends to the idea of treating others with kindness, compassion, and equity. It involves recognizing the interconnectedness of humanity and embracing a sense of social responsibility. Educators can instill a sense of justice in students by promoting empathy, teaching the importance of treating others with respect, and encouraging acts of kindness and altruism within the classroom and beyond.

Temperance (Sophrosyne)

Temperance, or self-control, is the virtue that enables individuals to govern their desires, impulses, and emotions. Stoics believe that excessive attachment to pleasure or avoidance of pain can lead to inner turmoil and hinder true happiness. In the classroom, educators can teach temperance by encouraging self-regulation, emotional awareness, and the practice of mindfulness. Helping students develop the ability to manage their emotions and impulses allows them to make better choices and maintain focus on their long-term goals.

The core Stoic values of wisdom, courage, justice, and temperance serve as powerful guiding principles for educators seeking to create a positive and growth-oriented classroom community. By integrating these virtues into the curriculum and daily interactions, educators can foster emotional intelligence, resilience, and virtuous behavior in their students. The cultivation of wisdom encourages critical thinking, while promoting courage instills a willingness to face challenges. Justice teaches empathy and social responsibility, and temperance empowers students to exercise self-control and make mindful decisions. As students embody these core Stoic values, they are better equipped to navigate life's complexities and cultivate a sense of purpose and fulfillment both inside and outside the classroom.

Applying Stoic Principles to Educational Settings

STOIC PRINCIPLES HOLD significant potential for transforming educational settings into nurturing environments that foster personal growth, emotional resilience, and a sense of purpose among students. By incorporating Stoic teachings into their teaching practices, educators can create a positive and impactful learning experience for their students.

Cultivating Emotional Resilience

Stoicism places great emphasis on understanding and managing emotions. In educational settings, cultivating emotional resilience is crucial for students to navigate the challenges of academic life effectively. By introducing Stoic practices such as mindfulness exercises, guided reflection, and journaling, educators can help students develop emotional intelligence and self-awareness. Encouraging students to recognize and process their feelings in a constructive manner equips them with the tools to cope with stress, setbacks, and emotional fluctuations, leading to a more positive and focused learning experience.

Emphasizing the Growth Mindset

The Stoic principle of the dichotomy of control teaches that some things are within our power, while others are not. Educators can use this concept to instill a growth mindset in their students, encouraging them to focus on their efforts, attitude, and response to challenges rather than feeling overwhelmed by external factors. By celebrating effort, perseverance, and the process of learning, students develop a greater sense of self-efficacy and motivation, which enhances their academic performance and fosters a love for learning.

Promoting Virtuous Behavior

Stoicism places a strong emphasis on the cultivation of virtues like wisdom, courage, justice, and temperance. In educational settings, educators can create a values-driven culture by integrating these virtues into the school's ethos and reinforcing them through character education programs. Encouraging students to act with integrity, empathy, and respect not only enhances classroom dynamics but also prepares them to become responsible and compassionate citizens.

Encouraging Stoic Reflection

Stoicism encourages regular self-reflection as a means to understand oneself better and make improvements in life. Educators can incorporate Stoic reflection practices, such as journaling or engaging in Socratic discussions, into the curriculum. By prompting students to contemplate their thoughts, actions, and values, educators help them develop self-awareness, critical thinking, and a deeper understanding of their emotions and behaviors.

Fostering a Supportive Classroom Community

Stoicism emphasizes the interconnectedness of all individuals and the importance of contributing positively to society. Educators can use this principle to promote a collaborative and supportive classroom community. By encouraging teamwork, cooperative learning, and open communication, students learn the value of empathy, respect for diverse perspectives, and the power of collective effort.

Teaching Resilience in the Face of Challenges

Stoicism teaches individuals to view challenges and setbacks as opportunities for growth rather than insurmountable obstacles. In educational settings, educators can use this Stoic perspective to encourage students to embrace difficulties as stepping stones to success. By providing guidance and support during difficult times, educators empower students to persevere and develop the tenacity needed to overcome obstacles both inside and outside the classroom.

Applying Stoic principles in educational settings offers a transformative approach to nurturing students' personal and academic development. By cultivating emotional resilience, promoting a growth mindset, encouraging virtuous behavior, and fostering a supportive classroom community, educators create an environment where students thrive emotionally, socially, and academically. Stoicism provides a practical and time-tested framework that empowers educators to cultivate well-rounded individuals who are prepared to face life's challenges with wisdom, courage, and inner tranquility. Through the application of Stoic principles, educational settings become not only places of learning but also spaces for personal growth and the cultivation of virtues that positively impact the lives of students.

III. Cultivating Empathy in the Classroom

Ἄνθρωπος δενδρεῖον, τοῖς καρποῖς αὐτοῦ γνωρίζεται.

A man's true value is shown in the fruits he bears.
(Meditations, 6.40)

---

*Ὑπὲρ σαυτοῦ μὴ ἔρχου, τίς γὰρ πολιτεύεται σῶς; πάντα μὲν οὖν τὰ
ἔθνη τῶν πόλεων ἕνεκεν ἐστίν, ἐκ τῶν δὲ πολιτῶν καὶ οἱ πόλεις.*

**Do not consider yourself to be the only one who is doing the
right thing; it is for this reason that cities exist, because
even from citizens they collect a combination of elements.**
(Meditations, 10.28)

Empathy as a Key Virtue in Stoicism

EMPATHY, THE ABILITY to understand and share the feelings of others, is a fundamental virtue in Stoicism. While Stoicism is often associated with emotional restraint, it does not imply indifference or a lack of compassion. On the contrary, Stoicism teaches individuals to cultivate empathy as a means to foster harmonious relationships, promote social cohesion, and contribute positively to the well-being of the community. In the classroom, cultivating empathy is not only essential for creating a supportive and inclusive learning environment but also aligns perfectly with the Stoic emphasis on virtuous behavior.

Understanding the Stoic Perspective on Empathy

Stoicism views empathy as an essential aspect of the human experience. By recognizing our shared humanity and interconnectedness, individuals develop a deeper sense of compassion and understanding toward others. The Stoics believed that empathy is not a passive emotion but an active virtue that drives individuals to act with kindness and consideration.

The Role of Empathy in Building Classroom Community

In educational settings, cultivating empathy is crucial for building a positive and cohesive classroom community. When students and educators practice empathy, they create an environment where each individual feels heard, valued, and respected. By understanding and appreciating each other's perspectives and experiences, students develop a sense of belonging and emotional safety, which enhances their willingness to participate, take risks, and collaborate with others.

Empathy and Conflict Resolution

Stoicism emphasizes the importance of resolving conflicts with reason and empathy. In the classroom, conflicts between students are inevitable, but empathy can be a powerful tool for de-escalating tense situations and finding mutually agreeable solutions. By teaching students to listen actively, acknowledge each other's feelings, and communicate with empathy, educators empower them with the skills needed to resolve conflicts constructively.

Empathy and Emotional Intelligence

Stoicism places a strong emphasis on emotional intelligence, which includes recognizing and understanding emotions in oneself and others. By cultivating empathy, students develop a heightened sense of emotional intelligence, which enables them to navigate social interactions with greater sensitivity and effectiveness. They become more adept at recognizing others' emotional cues, showing compassion, and responding appropriately to different emotional states.

Practicing Empathy Through Service and Kindness

Stoicism encourages individuals to practice empathy through acts of service and kindness. In the classroom, educators can incorporate service-learning projects or community service activities that allow students to connect with others outside their immediate circles.

Engaging in such activities not only promotes empathy but also fosters a sense of purpose and fulfillment as students contribute positively to their communities.

Empathy and Ethical Decision-Making

Empathy plays a vital role in ethical decision-making. When students put themselves in others' shoes and consider the consequences of their actions on others, they develop a strong moral compass aligned with Stoic values. Educators can encourage ethical discussions, case studies, and role-playing scenarios that challenge students to make empathetic and principled choices.

Empathy, as a key virtue in Stoicism, holds great significance in the educational setting. By cultivating empathy in the classroom, educators foster a compassionate and supportive community where students learn not only academic subjects but also essential life skills such as conflict resolution, emotional intelligence, and ethical decision-making. Stoicism's emphasis on empathy aligns perfectly with the goal of creating well-rounded individuals who are not only intellectually capable but also socially responsible and empathetic. Through the cultivation of empathy, the classroom becomes a place where students develop a deeper understanding of themselves and others, leading to greater emotional well-being, meaningful connections, and a sense of shared humanity.

Encouraging Open Communication and Active Listening

IN THE PURSUIT OF FOSTERING empathy within the classroom community, encouraging open communication and practicing active listening are indispensable tools. These practices not only create a supportive learning environment but also align closely with the Stoic emphasis on understanding and valuing the perspectives of others.

The Importance of Open Communication

Open communication is the cornerstone of a healthy and thriving classroom community. Encouraging students to express their thoughts, feelings, and concerns openly creates a safe space where they feel heard and respected. By promoting an environment of trust and open dialogue, educators set the stage for meaningful interactions and foster genuine connections among students.

Creating a Judgement-Free Zone

Stoicism teaches individuals to be nonjudgmental and understanding of others. Educators can apply this Stoic value by ensuring that the classroom is a judgment-free zone, where students are encouraged to share their ideas without fear of criticism or ridicule. When students feel accepted and valued for their contributions, they are more likely to engage actively in discussions and share their unique perspectives.

Teaching the Art of Active Listening

Active listening is a skill that empowers individuals to be fully present in a conversation, attentively absorbing the speaker's words and emotions. By teaching active listening techniques, such as maintaining eye contact, nodding, and paraphrasing, educators equip students with the ability to empathize with others. Active listening shows respect for the speaker and signals that their thoughts and feelings are being acknowledged.

Promoting Empathetic Language

In Stoicism, the words we use and the tone we employ are essential in fostering empathy and understanding. Educators can promote empathetic language by encouraging students to use "I" statements to express their feelings and by teaching them how to provide constructive feedback with sensitivity. By emphasizing the impact of words on others' emotions, educators promote effective communication and empathetic interactions.

Practicing Perspective Taking

Stoicism encourages individuals to consider the perspectives of others to foster understanding and empathy. In the classroom, educators can engage students in perspective-taking exercises, where they are asked to imagine themselves in someone else's situation or role-play different scenarios. These activities help students see situations from various viewpoints, enhancing their empathy and enriching their emotional intelligence.

Encouraging Empathy-Building Activities

To strengthen empathy within the classroom, educators can incorporate empathy-building activities into the curriculum. These may include reading and discussing literature that explores diverse experiences, engaging in role-playing exercises that address real-life situations, or participating in empathy-building games or simulations. Such activities enable students to step into the shoes of others and develop a deeper understanding of different perspectives.

Encouraging open communication and practicing active listening are pivotal in cultivating empathy within the classroom. By creating a supportive and nonjudgmental environment where students feel comfortable expressing themselves, educators foster meaningful connections and empathy among students. The Stoic emphasis on understanding and valuing the perspectives of others aligns seamlessly with the goal of nurturing empathy and emotional intelligence in students. Through open communication and active listening, students not only strengthen their interpersonal skills but also develop the ability to empathize, connect with others on a deeper level, and contribute positively to the classroom community and beyond.

Developing Emotional Intelligence in Students

EMOTIONAL INTELLIGENCE, the ability to recognize, understand, and manage one's emotions and those of others, is a crucial aspect of fostering empathy in the classroom. Stoicism places great emphasis on emotional intelligence as a means to achieve inner tranquility and harmonious relationships with others. By developing emotional intelligence in students, educators lay the foundation for creating a compassionate and empathetic learning environment.

Recognizing Emotions

The first step in developing emotional intelligence is to help students recognize and label their emotions accurately. Educators can teach students to identify different emotions and the physical sensations that accompany them. By providing a vocabulary to express emotions, students become better equipped to communicate their feelings effectively, allowing for more empathetic interactions.

Understanding the Impact of Emotions

Stoicism teaches that emotions are natural responses to external events, but they should not control our actions. Educators can help students understand the impact of emotions on their thoughts and behaviors. By exploring the connections between emotions, thoughts, and actions, students develop self-awareness and gain insight into how emotions influence their decision-making.

Cultivating Emotional Regulation

Stoicism advocates for mastering one's emotions rather than being controlled by them. Educators can teach students strategies for emotional regulation, such as deep breathing exercises, mindfulness practices, and finding healthy outlets for emotional expression. Learning to regulate emotions empowers students to respond to challenging situations with greater composure and empathy.

Developing Empathy Through Perspective-Taking

Stoicism emphasizes the importance of understanding the perspectives of others to foster empathy. Perspective-taking exercises in the classroom provide students with opportunities to step into others' shoes and see situations from different viewpoints. By encouraging students to consider the feelings and experiences of their peers, educators promote empathy and emotional intelligence.

Encouraging Empathetic Listening

Active listening, a key component of emotional intelligence, involves giving full attention to others and showing genuine interest in their experiences and emotions. Educators can model empathetic listening and provide opportunities for students to practice this skill during classroom discussions, group activities, and peer interactions.

Practicing Self-Compassion

Stoicism teaches individuals to be kind and compassionate toward themselves, recognizing that everyone is imperfect and prone to mistakes. Educators can foster self-compassion in students by promoting a growth mindset and emphasizing that setbacks are part of the learning process. When students learn to treat themselves with kindness and understanding, they are more likely to extend the same empathy to their peers.

Using Literature and Storytelling

Literature and storytelling offer valuable opportunities for students to explore emotions, empathy, and emotional intelligence. By reading books that feature diverse characters and emotional experiences, students gain insights into the human condition and develop a broader perspective on empathy and understanding.

Developing emotional intelligence in students is a vital aspect of cultivating empathy in the classroom. As educators teach students to recognize and understand their emotions, regulate their emotional responses, and empathize with others, they lay the groundwork for a compassionate and empathetic learning community. The Stoic principles of emotional self-mastery and perspective-taking align closely with the goal of nurturing emotional intelligence in students. Through the development of emotional intelligence, students become better equipped to navigate social interactions, show empathy and compassion toward others, and contribute positively to the classroom community and beyond.

IV. Nurturing Resilience Through Stoic Teachings

Non est ad astra mollis e terris via.

There is no easy way from the earth to the stars. *(Seneca, Hercules Furens, 437)*

Ἐλευθερίαν μόνην δεκτήν ἄξιον καὶ εἶναι, τὸ δὲ παρὰ ταῦτα ἀθρόως προσέχειν οὐκ ἄξιον.

Freedom is the only worthy goal in life. It is won by disregarding things that lie beyond our control. *(Discourses, 4.1.175)*

Τὰ γινόμενα πρὸς τὸν αὐτὸν σκοπὸν ἐποιοῦνται καὶ οὐχ ἡμῖν.

Events happen according to the same purpose, and not to us. *(Meditations, 5.8)*

Embracing Obstacles as Opportunities for Growth

RESILIENCE, THE ABILITY to bounce back from setbacks and adapt to challenging situations, is a valuable skill that Stoicism fosters in individuals. Embracing obstacles as opportunities for growth is a central tenet of Stoicism, teaching individuals to view adversity as a chance to develop inner strength and wisdom. In the classroom, nurturing resilience through Stoic teachings empowers students to face challenges with courage and determination, fostering a growth mindset and a positive outlook on learning and life.

Shifting Perspectives on Obstacles

Stoicism encourages individuals to reframe their perspective on obstacles. Instead of viewing challenges as insurmountable roadblocks, students are taught to see them as opportunities for learning and personal growth. By adopting this Stoic mindset, students develop a more positive and proactive approach to overcoming difficulties.

Developing the Dichotomy of Control

The dichotomy of control, a core concept in Stoicism, teaches individuals to focus their energy on what is within their control and let go of what is not. In the classroom, educators can use this principle to empower students to identify aspects of a challenge that they can influence and those beyond their control. This understanding helps students direct their efforts toward actionable solutions rather than becoming overwhelmed by factors outside their sphere of influence.

Practicing Acceptance and Adaptation

Stoicism emphasizes the importance of accepting the reality of a situation and adapting to it with grace and resilience. Educators can guide students in practicing acceptance by encouraging open discussions about challenges and setbacks. By accepting the circumstances they face, students can channel their energy into finding creative solutions and adapting their approach to achieve their goals.

Encouraging Perseverance and Grit

Stoicism teaches the value of perseverance and grit in the face of adversity. Students learn that setbacks are a natural part of the learning journey and that success often requires sustained effort and determination. By praising students' perseverance and recognizing their efforts, educators reinforce the Stoic principles of resilience and inner strength.

Using Stoic Role Models

Stoic history provides numerous role models who exemplify resilience in the face of challenges. Educators can introduce students to Stoic philosophers like Seneca, Epictetus, and Marcus Aurelius, sharing their stories of perseverance and determination. By learning from these Stoic role models, students can draw inspiration and wisdom to navigate their own obstacles with greater resilience.

Reflecting on Lessons Learned

Stoicism places emphasis on self-reflection and learning from experiences. Educators can incorporate reflective activities into the curriculum, allowing students to analyze their responses to challenges, identify lessons learned, and set goals for future growth. This practice not only reinforces resilience but also fosters a growth mindset and a sense of personal agency.

Nurturing resilience through Stoic teachings empowers students to view challenges as opportunities for growth and self-improvement. By adopting a Stoic mindset and embracing obstacles with courage and determination, students develop the resilience needed to face adversities in the classroom and beyond. The principles of the dichotomy of control, acceptance, and perseverance, as well as the inspiration from Stoic role models, provide a powerful framework for fostering resilience and inner strength in students. Through the cultivation of resilience, students become better equipped to navigate the ups and downs of the learning journey, embracing challenges as stepping stones to personal growth and success.

Fostering a Growth Mindset in Students

A GROWTH MINDSET, THE belief that one's abilities and intelligence can be developed through dedication and effort, is a foundational aspect of Stoic teachings. Stoicism emphasizes the power of our attitudes and responses to challenges, and fostering a growth mindset aligns perfectly with this Stoic perspective. By nurturing a growth mindset in students, educators empower them to embrace challenges, persist in the face of setbacks, and cultivate resilience in their academic and personal pursuits.

Emphasizing Effort and Process

Stoicism encourages individuals to focus on their efforts and actions rather than fixating on outcomes. In the classroom, educators can praise and celebrate students' hard work, determination, and perseverance, regardless of the immediate results. By emphasizing the value of effort and the learning process, students develop a growth mindset that embraces continuous improvement and sees failures as opportunities for learning and growth.

Challenging Limiting Beliefs

Stoicism challenges limiting beliefs that hinder personal development. Educators can help students identify and challenge their fixed mindset beliefs, such as "I'm not good at this" or "I'll never be able to do that." By encouraging students to reframe these beliefs and see challenges as opportunities to improve, educators foster a growth mindset that embraces challenges with confidence and curiosity.

Encouraging Risk-Taking

Stoicism encourages individuals to take calculated risks and step outside their comfort zones. In the classroom, educators can create a supportive environment where students feel safe to take risks and try new things without fear of judgment. By celebrating students' courage to take on challenges, educators reinforce the growth mindset that values the process of learning and improvement.

Celebrating Growth and Progress

Stoicism celebrates progress and self-improvement. Educators can highlight students' growth and accomplishments, no matter how small, to reinforce the idea that progress is a result of effort and dedication. By acknowledging and celebrating growth, students are motivated to continue their learning journey and maintain a positive outlook on their abilities.

Teaching the Power of Yet

The concept of "yet" is a powerful aspect of fostering a growth mindset. By adding the word "yet" to statements like "I don't understand this" or "I can't do this," students recognize that their current abilities are not fixed but can improve over time with effort and practice. This simple shift in language instills a sense of possibility and resilience in students.

Providing Constructive Feedback

Stoicism emphasizes the value of constructive criticism for personal growth. Educators can provide feedback that focuses on effort, improvement, and specific strategies for growth. By reframing feedback as an opportunity for learning and development, students become more receptive to challenges and view setbacks as chances to refine their skills.

Fostering a growth mindset in students is an essential component of nurturing resilience through Stoic teachings. By emphasizing effort and process, challenging limiting beliefs, encouraging risk-taking, and celebrating growth and progress, educators create a positive and empowering learning environment. The Stoic perspective aligns perfectly with the growth mindset, as both highlight the transformative power of attitude and effort in overcoming challenges. Through the cultivation of a growth mindset, students become more resilient, adaptable, and motivated to take on new challenges, embracing the Stoic philosophy that encourages continuous self-improvement and flourishing in all aspects of life.

Managing Setbacks and Failures Using Stoic Techniques

SETBACKS AND FAILURES are inevitable in life, and Stoicism offers valuable techniques for managing and responding to these challenges in a constructive and resilient manner. By teaching students Stoic techniques to navigate setbacks, educators empower them to develop emotional strength, maintain a positive mindset, and grow from adversity.

Practicing Acceptance of the Uncontrollable

Stoicism teaches individuals to recognize and accept that some things are beyond their control. In the face of setbacks and failures, educators can guide students to differentiate between what they can change and what they cannot. By accepting the reality of the situation and focusing their energy on the controllable aspects, students develop resilience and avoid feelings of helplessness.

Applying the Dichotomy of Control

The dichotomy of control, a fundamental Stoic concept, encourages individuals to focus on their thoughts, attitudes, and actions rather than external events. When students encounter setbacks, educators can remind them to apply this Stoic principle and concentrate on their response to the situation. By shifting the focus to what they can control, students develop a sense of agency and personal responsibility in the face of challenges.

Reframing Failures as Learning Opportunities

Stoicism encourages individuals to reframe failures as opportunities for learning and growth. Educators can help students view setbacks as valuable experiences that offer insights for improvement. By discussing the lessons to be learned from failures and highlighting historical examples of resilience in the face of adversity, students develop a growth mindset that embraces setbacks as stepping stones to success.

Engaging in Stoic Reflection

Stoic reflection, such as journaling or guided self-inquiry, provides students with an outlet to process their emotions and thoughts about setbacks. Educators can encourage students to engage in Stoic reflection exercises to gain clarity, identify their emotions, and challenge unhelpful beliefs. Stoic reflection fosters self-awareness and emotional intelligence, empowering students to respond to setbacks with greater self-control.

Cultivating Stoic Resilience Exercises

Stoicism offers practical resilience exercises that educators can introduce in the classroom. For example, the "Premeditation of Adversity" exercise involves students imagining potential setbacks and planning how they would handle them calmly and rationally. The "View from Above" exercise encourages students to take a broader perspective on their setbacks, recognizing their temporary nature in the grand scheme of life.

Encouraging Supportive Peer Relationships

Stoicism emphasizes the importance of community and interconnectedness. Educators can foster a supportive classroom community where students feel comfortable sharing their setbacks and offering support to their peers. Encouraging empathy and compassion among students helps create a safe space for vulnerability and growth.

Managing setbacks and failures using Stoic techniques equips students with the tools to navigate challenges with resilience and wisdom. By practicing acceptance, applying the dichotomy of control, reframing failures, engaging in Stoic reflection, and cultivating Stoic resilience exercises, students develop the emotional strength to face setbacks constructively. Stoicism's emphasis on personal agency, growth, and community aligns seamlessly with the goal of nurturing resilience in the face of adversity. Through Stoic techniques, students not only build resilience but also cultivate a deeper understanding of themselves and the world, leading to personal growth, inner tranquility, and a positive outlook on their academic and life journey.

V. Promoting Positive Interactions

Ὁ σοφὸς ἀγαθὸς καὶ παρὰ τοῖς ἀνθρώποις ἀγαθός.

The wise man is good, and good also in the eyes of others.
(*Discourses, 3.22.48*)

Πρὸς τοὺς τοιούτους, ὅσοις μὴ διὰ φιλοστοργίας καὶ φιλανθρωπίας ἀλλὰ δι' ἀσεβείας καὶ ἀδικίας περιπίπτουσιν, οὐ χρή σε αὐτοὺς ἀποτρέπειν ἀλλ' ἐπιπατεῖν.

Treat those who cause harm not with aversion but with compassion and understanding. (*Meditations, 11.18*)

Fostering Kindness and Compassion Among Students

KINDNESS AND COMPASSION lie at the heart of Stoic teachings, reflecting the philosophy's emphasis on virtuous behavior and the interconnectedness of humanity. In the classroom, fostering kindness and compassion among students creates a nurturing and supportive learning environment where individuals feel valued, respected, and understood. By incorporating Stoic principles of benevolence and empathy, educators promote positive interactions that enhance the overall classroom community.

Leading by Example

Educators play a pivotal role in fostering kindness and compassion among students by leading by example. Demonstrating empathy, understanding, and respect in their interactions with students sets a positive tone for the classroom community. By modeling compassionate behavior, educators encourage students to emulate these virtues in their own interactions with peers and teachers.

Encouraging Acts of Kindness

Stoicism teaches that acts of kindness, no matter how small, have a positive ripple effect on the well-being of others and the community as a whole. Educators can create opportunities for students to engage in acts of kindness, such as helping a classmate, offering encouragement, or showing appreciation for each other's efforts. By acknowledging and celebrating these acts, educators reinforce the value of kindness and its impact on the classroom environment.

Building a Culture of Empathy

Empathy is a core Stoic virtue that nurtures a sense of shared humanity and understanding. Educators can cultivate empathy in the classroom by incorporating empathy-building activities, such as perspective-taking exercises, discussions on diverse experiences, and reading literature that explores emotions and interpersonal connections. As students develop empathy, they become more compassionate and considerate in their interactions with others.

Addressing Bullying and Conflict with Compassion

Stoicism advocates for resolving conflicts with reason and compassion. When addressing bullying or conflicts in the classroom, educators can create a safe space for open communication and encourage empathy in conflict resolution. By teaching students to approach disagreements with understanding and kindness, educators promote positive conflict resolution skills and foster a culture of respect and cooperation.

Recognizing Acts of Compassion

Incorporating Stoic principles, educators can recognize and reward acts of compassion and kindness. Celebrating instances of empathy and benevolence reinforces the importance of these virtues within the classroom community. By highlighting compassionate behavior, educators encourage students to continue displaying acts of kindness, creating a positive feedback loop of virtuous behavior.

Incorporating Service-Learning Projects

Stoicism emphasizes the value of contributing positively to society and the well-being of others. Educators can organize service-learning projects that allow students to engage with the community and address social issues with empathy and compassion. Service-learning experiences not only promote kindness and compassion but also instill a sense of purpose and fulfillment in students as they recognize the impact of their actions on others.

Fostering kindness and compassion among students in the classroom aligns harmoniously with Stoic principles and creates a positive and supportive learning environment. By leading by example, encouraging acts of kindness, building a culture of empathy, addressing conflicts with compassion, recognizing acts of benevolence, and incorporating service-learning projects, educators empower students to embrace the Stoic virtues of kindness and compassion. The cultivation of these virtues not only enhances the classroom community but also equips students with essential interpersonal skills that extend beyond the classroom into their future roles as compassionate and empathetic members of society.

Emphasizing the Importance of Cooperation Over Competition

STOICISM PLACES GREAT value on fostering harmonious relationships and recognizing the interconnectedness of humanity. In the classroom, emphasizing the importance of cooperation over competition aligns closely with Stoic principles, creating a supportive and collaborative learning environment that nurtures empathy, respect, and mutual growth among students.

Shifting the Focus from Competition to Collaboration

In a competitive culture, students may feel pressured to outperform others, leading to stress and a sense of isolation. Educators can emphasize cooperation over competition by shifting the focus from individual achievement to collaborative efforts. By encouraging teamwork, group projects, and peer support, educators create a learning environment that promotes cooperation and values collective success.

Teaching the Stoic Concept of the Common Good

Stoicism emphasizes the pursuit of the common good, recognizing that the well-being of individuals is interconnected with the welfare of the community. Educators can introduce the Stoic concept of the common good to students, explaining how cooperation benefits not only individuals but also the entire classroom community. By fostering a sense of collective responsibility, students learn to support and uplift one another.

Encouraging Peer Tutoring and Mentoring

Peer tutoring and mentoring provide opportunities for students to help and learn from each other. By encouraging students to share their knowledge and skills with their peers, educators promote cooperation and strengthen interpersonal relationships. Students who engage in peer tutoring gain a deeper understanding of the subject matter while building empathy and leadership skills.

Creating a Culture of Support and Encouragement

In a cooperative classroom culture, students feel comfortable seeking help and offering support to their peers. Educators can create a supportive atmosphere by encouraging students to ask questions, collaborate on problem-solving, and offer encouragement to one another. This culture of support builds trust among students and fosters a sense of belonging.

Recognizing Collective Achievements

Stoicism teaches individuals to celebrate the achievements of the group rather than seeking individual accolades. Educators can reinforce this Stoic principle by recognizing and celebrating collective achievements in the classroom. Whether it's a successful group project, a collaborative effort, or a cooperative learning experience, acknowledging the contributions of the entire class reinforces the importance of cooperation and teamwork.

Facilitating Discussions on Interdependence

Stoicism highlights the interconnectedness of all individuals, and educators can facilitate discussions on interdependence and the significance of working together as a community. By exploring the consequences of both competitive and cooperative approaches to learning and problem-solving, students gain insights into the benefits of cooperation and empathy.

Emphasizing the importance of cooperation over competition in the classroom promotes a nurturing and supportive learning environment that aligns perfectly with Stoic principles. By shifting the focus from individual success to collective growth, educators foster a sense of community and interdependence among students. Through peer tutoring, mentoring, and collaboration, students learn the value of cooperation, empathy, and shared success. The Stoic concept of the common good reinforces the idea that the well-being of individuals is intertwined with the welfare of the group. By promoting positive interactions grounded in cooperation and teamwork, educators equip students with essential interpersonal skills that extend beyond the classroom, preparing them to contribute positively to society and embody the Stoic ideals of harmonious relationships and shared purpose.

Creating a Culture of Respect and Inclusivity

A CULTURE OF RESPECT and inclusivity is central to Stoicism, which emphasizes the inherent worth and dignity of all individuals. In the classroom, creating such a culture fosters empathy, understanding, and a sense of belonging among students. By incorporating Stoic principles of treating others with kindness and recognizing the interconnectedness of humanity, educators promote positive interactions that celebrate diversity and build a supportive learning community.

Establishing Clear Expectations for Respect

Educators play a crucial role in setting the tone for a respectful classroom culture. By establishing clear expectations for respectful behavior and communication, educators create a safe and inclusive environment where all students feel valued and heard. Modeling respectful interactions and addressing any instances of disrespect promptly reinforces the importance of treating others with dignity.

Promoting Active Listening and Open Communication

Stoicism values the skill of active listening, which involves giving full attention to others and seeking to understand their perspectives. Educators can encourage active listening through classroom discussions, group activities, and one-on-one interactions. By promoting open communication, students learn to appreciate diverse viewpoints and engage in constructive dialogue.

Addressing Bias and Prejudice

Stoicism rejects discrimination and prejudice, emphasizing the equality of all individuals. Educators can address bias and prejudice by incorporating diversity and inclusion discussions into the curriculum. By exploring topics related to identity, culture, and social justice, students gain awareness of their biases and learn to foster an inclusive environment.

Encouraging Empathy and Perspective-Taking

Stoicism places great importance on empathy and understanding the perspectives of others. Educators can encourage empathy through perspective-taking exercises and discussions on diverse experiences. By fostering an understanding of different viewpoints, students develop compassion and respect for the unique backgrounds and identities of their peers.

Implementing Restorative Practices

Stoicism acknowledges the power of forgiveness and second chances. In the classroom, educators can implement restorative practices to address conflicts and harmful behavior. Restorative approaches focus on repairing harm, promoting empathy, and restoring relationships, reinforcing the value of respect and inclusivity.

Creating Opportunities for Student Input

Inclusive classrooms involve students in decision-making and value their input. Educators can create opportunities for student voice and choice in classroom activities, projects, and discussions. By valuing each student's contributions, educators promote a culture where diverse perspectives are embraced and respected.

Celebrating Diversity and Cultural Awareness

Stoicism recognizes the beauty of human diversity and the richness of different cultures. Educators can celebrate diversity and promote cultural awareness through multicultural events, literature, and guest speakers. By highlighting the contributions of various cultures, students develop a broader understanding of the world and a sense of global citizenship.

Creating a culture of respect and inclusivity in the classroom aligns harmoniously with Stoic principles, promoting positive interactions and nurturing a supportive learning environment. By establishing clear expectations for respect, promoting active listening and empathy, addressing bias and prejudice, and implementing restorative practices, educators foster a sense of belonging and mutual understanding among students. A culture that values student input, celebrates diversity, and promotes cultural awareness aligns with Stoic ideals of treating others with dignity and recognizing the interconnectedness of humanity. Through the cultivation of respect and inclusivity, educators prepare students to be compassionate and empathetic individuals, equipped to contribute positively to their classrooms, communities, and the world at large.

VI. Mindfulness and Self-Reflection

———

Κατάμαθε πάντα, πεπραγμένα καὶ μέλλοντα, μὴ πάσχειν μόνον, ἀλλὰ καὶ πράττειν, καὶ τοῦτο ἐστὶ φροντίζειν.

Examine your actions in relation to everything, past and future, and don't suffer only, but also act; that's what it means to care for yourself. *(Enchiridion, 19)*

———

Οὐ πάθει πολλῷ ὁ ἄνθρωπος, ὅσῳ ἐνόμισεν, ἀλλ' ὅσῳ δοκεῖ πάθος ἐπάθη.

Man is not worried by real problems so much as by his imagined anxieties about real problems. *(Enchiridion, 5)*

Integrating Mindfulness Practices into the Classroom Routine

MINDFULNESS, THE PRACTICE of being fully present and aware of one's thoughts, emotions, and surroundings, is a core aspect of Stoicism. Integrating mindfulness practices into the classroom routine offers numerous benefits, including improved focus, emotional regulation, and self-awareness. By incorporating Stoic principles of self-reflection and living in the present moment, educators create a calmer and more centered learning environment that promotes overall well-being and academic success.

Mindful Start and End of the Day

Begin and end each school day with a mindful moment. Gather students in a circle or at their desks and guide them through a brief mindfulness exercise. This may involve deep breathing, body scans, or simply taking a few moments to sit quietly and focus on their breath. Starting and ending the day mindfully helps students transition into a focused and present state of mind.

Mindful Transitions between Activities

Use mindfulness practices during transitions between activities. For example, before starting a new lesson or moving to a different subject, lead students in a short mindfulness exercise to help them refocus their attention and approach the new task with a clear and calm mind.

Mindful Listening and Observing

Incorporate mindfulness into classroom discussions and activities by encouraging mindful listening and observing. Before starting a class discussion, remind students to listen attentively to their peers and to be fully present in the conversation. During activities, encourage students to notice the details of their surroundings and engage their senses mindfully.

Mindful Breathing During Stressful Moments

Teach students to use mindful breathing as a tool to manage stress and regulate emotions. When students encounter challenging situations or feel overwhelmed, they can practice deep breathing to center themselves and approach the situation with composure and clarity.

Mindful Reflection Journals

Introduce mindful reflection journals where students can write about their thoughts, feelings, and experiences in a nonjudgmental and introspective way. Encourage students to use their journals for self-reflection and to explore how they can apply Stoic principles in their daily lives.

Gratitude and Mindful Appreciation

Stoicism emphasizes the practice of gratitude, and educators can integrate mindful appreciation exercises into the classroom routine. Encourage students to take a moment each day to reflect on things they are grateful for, fostering a positive and appreciative mindset.

Mindful Movement and Stretching

Incorporate mindful movement and stretching exercises into the classroom routine to promote physical and mental well-being. Guided stretching or yoga sessions can help students relax, release tension, and become more aware of their bodies.

Integrating mindfulness practices into the classroom routine aligns closely with Stoic principles of self-awareness, present moment awareness, and self-reflection. By incorporating mindful moments at the start and end of the day, during transitions, and during class activities, educators create a calm and focused learning environment that enhances students' overall well-being and academic performance. Mindfulness helps students develop self-regulation skills, emotional intelligence, and a deeper understanding of themselves and others. By nurturing mindfulness in the classroom, educators equip students with valuable tools for navigating life's challenges and cultivating a sense of inner peace and resilience grounded in Stoic wisdom.

Guided Self-Reflection Exercises for Students

GUIDED SELF-REFLECTION exercises offer valuable opportunities for students to explore their thoughts, emotions, and actions in a Stoic context. Through these exercises, students develop self-awareness, emotional intelligence, and a deeper understanding of Stoic principles. Guided self-reflection helps students apply Stoic teachings to their daily lives, fostering personal growth, and enriching their learning journey.

The Stoic Journal

Encourage students to keep a Stoic journal where they can record their thoughts and reflections on various aspects of their lives. Provide guided prompts that relate to Stoic principles, such as:

- How did you respond to a recent challenge or setback, and how could you have applied Stoic principles in your response?
- Reflect on a situation where you practiced empathy and understanding towards others. How did this align with Stoic

virtues?

- Describe a time when you faced a difficult decision. How could you have applied the dichotomy of control in this situation?

Daily Stoic Affirmations

Introduce daily Stoic affirmations for students to recite at the beginning or end of each day. These affirmations can focus on key Stoic virtues such as wisdom, courage, justice, and temperance. For example:

- "I will embrace challenges as opportunities for growth and learning."
- "I will approach setbacks with resilience and a growth mindset."
- "I will show empathy and compassion towards others, recognizing our shared humanity."

The Stoic Question of the Day

Pose a Stoic question of the day to prompt class discussions and individual reflections. Questions may revolve around Stoic values, ethical dilemmas, or applying Stoic teachings to real-life situations. For example:

- "How can the Stoic principle of living in accordance with nature guide our actions in preserving the environment?"
- "In what ways can we practice self-discipline and temperance in our daily habits?"
- "Discuss how the Stoic concept of the common good applies to current social issues."

The Stoic Virtue Cards

Create sets of virtue cards representing Stoic virtues such as wisdom, courage, justice, and temperance. Each card can have a virtue on one side and an example of its application on the other. Students can draw a card and reflect on how they can embody that virtue throughout the day.

The Stoic Reflection Circle

Organize a Stoic reflection circle where students can share their insights and reflections based on Stoic teachings. In a safe and supportive environment, students can discuss their experiences, challenges, and successes in applying Stoic principles. The reflection circle encourages open dialogue and promotes a sense of community based on Stoic values.

The Stoic Virtue Portrait

Have students create visual representations of Stoic virtues through art, photography, or multimedia projects. These virtue portraits can illustrate how each virtue is exemplified in real-life scenarios or historical figures who embodied Stoic ideals. Through creative expression, students deepen their understanding of Stoic virtues and their relevance in various contexts.

Guided self-reflection exercises for students enable them to engage actively with Stoic principles and apply them to their lives. By using journals, affirmations, questions, virtue cards, reflection circles, and virtue portraits, educators facilitate meaningful self-exploration and promote the development of emotional intelligence and resilience grounded in Stoic wisdom. Guided self-reflection empowers students to cultivate self-awareness, ethical reasoning, and a sense of purpose aligned with Stoic values. Through these exercises, students gain practical insights into Stoicism's relevance in their daily lives and its potential to foster personal growth, mindfulness, and a deeper appreciation for the interconnectedness of all humanity.

Encouraging Journaling and Introspection

ENCOURAGING JOURNALING and introspection in the classroom provides students with a powerful means to explore their thoughts, feelings, and experiences through a Stoic lens. Journaling fosters self-awareness, emotional intelligence, and critical thinking, aligning perfectly with Stoic principles of self-reflection and inner tranquility. By incorporating journaling and introspection into the learning process, educators empower students to deepen their understanding of Stoicism and its application in their lives.

Daily Stoic Reflections

Encourage students to engage in daily Stoic reflections in their journals. At the beginning or end of each day, students can write about their experiences, challenges, and successes in applying Stoic principles. Prompts may include:

- How did you exhibit wisdom, courage, justice, or temperance today?

- Reflect on a situation where you practiced empathy and understanding towards others.
- Describe a recent obstacle you faced and how you applied Stoic teachings to navigate it.

Stoic Quotes and Insights

Provide students with Stoic quotes and passages to inspire their journaling. Students can select quotes that resonate with them and explore their personal interpretations and reflections on the Stoic wisdom contained within the words. Encourage them to relate the quotes to their own experiences and explore the practical implications of Stoicism in their lives.

Stoic Philosophical Exercises

Introduce Stoic philosophical exercises that prompt deeper introspection. For example, students can engage in the "View from Above" exercise, where they imagine themselves viewing their current situation from a cosmic perspective. This exercise helps students gain a sense of perspective and humility, recognizing the impermanence of their challenges.

Virtue Analysis

Encourage students to explore the Stoic virtues of wisdom, courage, justice, and temperance in their journal entries. They can reflect on how they embody these virtues in their daily lives and consider areas for improvement. By analyzing their actions through the lens of Stoic virtues, students develop a deeper understanding of ethical decision-making.

Letters to Self

Encourage students to write letters to their future selves, reflecting on their growth, values, and aspirations. By engaging in this form of self-reflection, students gain clarity on their long-term goals and how they can apply Stoic principles to achieve personal fulfillment and virtue.

Mindful Gratitude Journaling

Incorporate mindful gratitude journaling into the classroom routine. Students can write about things they are grateful for, focusing on the Stoic concept of recognizing and appreciating the blessings in their lives, no matter how small.

Stoic Lessons from Literature

Integrate literature that contains Stoic themes into the curriculum. After reading relevant passages or stories, encourage students to reflect on the Stoic lessons and insights present in the texts. They can connect these lessons to their own lives and consider how the characters' experiences mirror Stoic teachings.

Encouraging journaling and introspection in the classroom provides a valuable platform for students to explore Stoic principles and their personal growth journey. By engaging in daily reflections, analyzing Stoic quotes, and participating in philosophical exercises, students develop a deeper understanding of Stoicism and its practical application in their lives. Journaling allows students to explore their thoughts, emotions, and actions through a Stoic lens, fostering self-awareness, empathy, and ethical reasoning. The incorporation of mindful gratitude journaling and Stoic lessons from literature enhances students' sense of appreciation and connection to the Stoic philosophy. By encouraging journaling and introspection, educators support students in developing the critical skills needed to live a virtuous and fulfilling life, grounded in Stoic wisdom and self-reflection.

VII. Building Trust and Community Engagement

Τὸ ζῆν γὰρ οὐκ ἔστι τὸ σῶμα, ἀλλὰ τὸ εὖ ζῆν.

For living is not being alive, but living well. *(Meditations, 5.16)*

Τὸ ζῆν κοινὸν τοῖς ἀνθρώποις, τὸ δὲ κοινωνεῖν λόγον κοινωνία.

The fact that human life is shared, and that to share is to speak, is what gives rise to community. *(Meditations, 8.55)*

Establishing a Safe and Trusting Learning Environment

ESTABLISHING A SAFE and trusting learning environment is fundamental to fostering a positive classroom community grounded in Stoic principles. A classroom where students feel safe to express themselves, take risks, and learn from failures promotes emotional well-being and academic growth. By cultivating trust among students and between students and educators, the classroom becomes a supportive space for collaborative learning, empathy, and personal development.

Cultivate Positive Relationships

Forge positive relationships with each student by getting to know them individually. Show genuine interest in their interests, passions, and concerns. As educators build authentic connections with students, they create a foundation of trust and mutual respect that underpins the entire learning environment.

Embrace Vulnerability

Model vulnerability and openness as an educator, sharing personal stories of challenges, failures, and growth. When students see their teachers embracing vulnerability, they feel more comfortable being authentic and vulnerable themselves, fostering a sense of safety and belonging in the classroom.

Set Clear Expectations

Establish clear and consistent expectations for behavior, communication, and mutual respect in the classroom. By setting boundaries and guidelines, educators create a structured environment where students feel secure and know what is expected of them.

Encourage Positive Communication

Promote positive and constructive communication in the classroom. Teach students effective communication skills, including active listening and respectful expression of ideas and emotions. Encourage open dialogue and empathy, helping students learn from diverse perspectives and build a sense of community.

Address Conflict with Empathy

Conflict is a natural part of human interactions. When conflicts arise, address them with empathy and a focus on understanding all perspectives involved. Guide students in resolving conflicts through active listening, communication, and seeking common ground.

Recognize Effort and Progress

Celebrate students' efforts and progress, no matter how small. Recognize their achievements and growth, reinforcing the idea that the learning journey is as important as the final outcomes. This recognition creates a positive and encouraging atmosphere that motivates students to continue striving for excellence.

Create Inclusive Learning Opportunities

Design learning experiences that promote collaboration and inclusivity. Group projects, discussions, and cooperative activities provide opportunities for students to work together, value each other's contributions, and appreciate diverse perspectives.

Establish Classroom Norms Together

Involve students in creating classroom norms and rules. When students have a voice in establishing the norms, they feel a sense of ownership and responsibility for maintaining a respectful and safe environment.

Establishing a safe and trusting learning environment in the classroom is essential for fostering a positive community grounded in Stoic principles. By cultivating positive relationships, embracing vulnerability, setting clear expectations, encouraging positive communication, addressing conflict with empathy, recognizing effort and progress, creating inclusive learning opportunities, and establishing classroom norms together, educators create an environment where students feel valued, respected, and supported. A safe and trusting learning environment promotes emotional well-being, empathy, and collaboration, laying the groundwork for students to embrace Stoic virtues in their interactions with others and their personal growth journey. By building trust and community engagement, educators pave the way for students to flourish academically, emotionally, and ethically, embodying Stoicism's emphasis on interconnectedness and the pursuit of virtuous living.

Engaging Parents and Caregivers in the Community-Building Process

INVOLVING PARENTS AND caregivers in the community-building process is crucial for creating a holistic and supportive learning environment that aligns with Stoic principles. When educators and families work together, students benefit from consistent messages, shared values, and a strong support network. Engaging parents and caregivers fosters trust, open communication, and a shared commitment to the well-being and growth of the students.

Welcome and Orientation Meetings

At the beginning of the school year or semester, hold welcome and orientation meetings where parents and caregivers can meet the educators and learn about the classroom's community-building efforts. During these meetings, share information about the classroom's approach to fostering trust, empathy, and collaboration based on Stoic principles.

Collaborative Goal-Setting

Encourage parents and caregivers to actively participate in goal-setting for their children's academic and personal development. Collaborative goal-setting involves open dialogue between educators, parents, and caregivers to establish shared objectives that encompass both academic achievements and character development in line with Stoic virtues.

Communicate Classroom Values

Regularly communicate classroom values and community-building initiatives to parents and caregivers through newsletters, emails, or dedicated communication platforms. Share insights into the Stoic philosophy and how it informs classroom practices, fostering transparency and alignment between home and school environments.

Parent Workshops on Stoic Principles

Organize workshops or information sessions for parents and caregivers on Stoic principles and their relevance to education and child development. By educating parents about Stoicism, they can better understand the philosophy's impact on their children's learning experiences and character development.

Involvement in Community Activities

Encourage parents and caregivers to participate in community activities that promote trust and engagement, such as school events, volunteer opportunities, or parent-teacher conferences. These interactions provide valuable opportunities for educators and families to build meaningful connections and collaborate in nurturing the students' growth.

Encourage Feedback and Input

Invite parents and caregivers to provide feedback and input on community-building efforts and classroom practices. By actively seeking their perspectives, educators demonstrate their commitment to fostering a collaborative and inclusive learning environment.

Recognize Parent Contributions

Recognize and appreciate the contributions of parents and caregivers in the community-building process. Celebrate their involvement, support, and collaboration, reinforcing the idea that a strong partnership between educators and families enhances the overall well-being and success of the students.

Address Challenges Together

In cases of challenges or concerns, approach parents and caregivers with empathy and a problem-solving mindset. By working together to address difficulties, educators and families demonstrate a shared commitment to supporting the students' emotional and academic growth.

Engaging parents and caregivers in the community-building process is essential for creating a cohesive and supportive learning environment rooted in Stoic principles. By involving families in collaborative goal-setting, communicating classroom values, organizing workshops on Stoic principles, and encouraging involvement in community activities, educators foster trust, open communication, and a shared commitment to the well-being and growth of the students. The partnership between educators and families promotes consistency between home and school environments, allowing students to experience a seamless integration of Stoic virtues in their daily lives. By recognizing parent contributions, seeking their input, and addressing challenges together, educators strengthen the community's foundation and create a supportive network that enhances students' emotional resilience and academic success. The active engagement of parents and caregivers in the community-building process aligns with Stoicism's emphasis on interconnectedness and the shared pursuit of virtuous living for the holistic development of each student.

Collaborative Projects and Activities to Strengthen the Classroom Community

COLLABORATIVE PROJECTS and activities play a vital role in strengthening the classroom community by promoting teamwork, empathy, and a shared sense of purpose. By incorporating Stoic principles of interdependence and the pursuit of the common good, educators create opportunities for students to engage actively with one another and build lasting connections. These collaborative endeavors foster a sense of belonging and camaraderie, enhancing the overall learning experience and fostering the development of essential life skills.

Community Service Projects

Organize community service projects that allow students to give back to their local community. Working together for a common cause nurtures a sense of empathy, compassion, and social responsibility. Students experience firsthand the impact of their collective efforts, fostering a deeper connection to one another and the broader community.

Group Discussions on Stoic Ethics

Facilitate group discussions on Stoic ethics and values, where students can explore how Stoicism applies to their lives and interactions with others. Discussing Stoic principles such as wisdom, courage, justice, and temperance in a collaborative setting deepens students' understanding and encourages them to practice these virtues in their daily lives.

Collaborative Art or Creative Projects

Encourage collaborative art or creative projects where students can work together to express Stoic concepts through various artistic mediums. Artistic collaboration fosters teamwork, communication, and a sense of shared creativity while reinforcing the Stoic idea of interconnectedness and unity.

Group Problem-Solving Challenges

Design group problem-solving challenges that require students to work together to overcome obstacles and find solutions. These challenges may include puzzles, brain teasers, or real-life scenarios that encourage students to apply critical thinking, communication, and cooperation in pursuit of shared goals.

Classroom Circle of Appreciation

Incorporate a "Circle of Appreciation" activity, where students take turns expressing gratitude and appreciation for their classmates' contributions, kindness, or helpfulness. This activity reinforces the importance of recognizing and valuing one another's efforts, fostering a positive and supportive classroom atmosphere.

Collaborative Book Clubs

Form collaborative book clubs where students read and discuss literature related to Stoicism and its practical application. Encourage students to share their insights, reflections, and how they see Stoic principles manifesting in the characters and themes of the books.

Building a Stoic Community Creed

Involve students in creating a Stoic community creed that outlines shared values and aspirations based on Stoic principles. Students can collaboratively develop the creed and take ownership of living by its guiding principles in their interactions with one another.

Celebrating Cultural Diversity

Organize activities that celebrate the cultural diversity within the classroom community. Students can share aspects of their cultural backgrounds, traditions, and experiences, fostering understanding, empathy, and appreciation for one another's uniqueness.

Collaborative projects and activities play a significant role in strengthening the classroom community through shared experiences and cooperative learning. By engaging in community service projects, group discussions on Stoic ethics, collaborative art projects, and group problem-solving challenges, students develop teamwork skills, empathy, and a sense of interconnectedness grounded in Stoic principles. The inclusion of classroom circles of appreciation, collaborative book clubs, and the creation of a Stoic community creed reinforces the values of mutual respect, gratitude, and shared aspirations. Celebrating cultural diversity fosters an inclusive environment where students appreciate each other's backgrounds and perspectives. Through these collaborative endeavors, educators create a classroom community that embodies Stoic ideals of interdependence, the pursuit of the common good, and the cultivation of virtue. The bonds formed through collaborative projects and activities deepen students' connections with one another, contributing to a supportive and positive learning environment where students thrive academically, socially, and emotionally.

VIII. Managing Conflicts and Challenges

Τὸ κάλλιστον μὲν ἐστὶν οὐ μιμεῖσθαι τὸν ποιήσαντα, ἀλλὰ ἀντίκρυ οὕτως ὡς ἐκεῖνον.

The best revenge is to be unlike the one who performed the injury. *(Meditations, 6.60)*

Aequam memento rebus in arduis servare mentem.

Remember to keep a calm mind in difficult situations.
(Seneca, Hercules Furens, 235)

Using Stoic Techniques for Conflict Resolution

CONFLICT RESOLUTION is an essential skill for students to develop, and Stoic techniques offer valuable tools for addressing conflicts with wisdom and compassion. By incorporating Stoic principles of self-control, empathy, and the pursuit of virtue, educators empower students to navigate conflicts in a constructive and empathetic manner. These Stoic techniques promote personal growth, strengthen relationships, and foster a harmonious learning environment.

Pause and Reflect

Encourage students to pause and take a moment to reflect before responding to a conflict. In the heat of the moment, emotions can cloud judgment and lead to impulsive reactions. Stoicism teaches the value of self-control and the ability to pause, reflect, and approach conflicts with a clear and rational mindset.

Focus on What Is Within Your Control

Stoicism emphasizes focusing on what is within our control and accepting what is not. During conflicts, students can apply this principle by identifying what they can influence or change and what they cannot. By directing their energy towards solutions rather than dwelling on the uncontrollable, students can approach conflict resolution with a calmer and more constructive mindset.

Practice Empathy and Perspective-Taking

Stoicism encourages empathy and understanding the perspectives of others. When facing conflicts, students can practice empathy by considering the feelings and motivations of all parties involved. By putting themselves in others' shoes, students develop a deeper appreciation for the complexity of human emotions and experiences, fostering more compassionate and effective conflict resolution.

Seek Common Ground

Stoicism teaches that humans are inherently social beings, emphasizing the importance of finding common ground and building connections. Encourage students to seek common interests or shared goals during conflicts, promoting collaboration and mutual understanding. By focusing on shared objectives, students can work together to find solutions that benefit everyone involved.

Reframe Perspectives

Help students reframe their perspectives during conflicts. Stoicism encourages viewing challenges as opportunities for growth and learning. By reframing conflicts as chances to develop resilience, problem-solving skills, and emotional intelligence, students approach conflicts with a growth mindset, which can lead to more positive outcomes.

Practice Forgiveness

Stoicism highlights the power of forgiveness and the importance of letting go of anger and resentment. Encourage students to practice forgiveness as a way to release emotional burdens and move towards resolution. This Stoic technique fosters healing and allows students to focus on building positive relationships.

Focus on Virtuous Action

Encourage students to focus on virtuous action during conflicts, aligning their responses with Stoic values of wisdom, courage, justice, and temperance. By striving to act virtuously, students can navigate conflicts with integrity and uphold their ethical principles, even in challenging situations.

Implement Mediation and Dialogue

Introduce mediation and dialogue as Stoic techniques for resolving conflicts. Mediation involves a neutral third party helping parties in conflict find common ground and reach an agreement. Dialogue encourages open communication and active listening, fostering understanding and collaboration.

Using Stoic techniques for conflict resolution empowers students to approach conflicts with mindfulness, empathy, and wisdom. By pausing and reflecting, focusing on what is within their control, practicing empathy, seeking common ground, reframing perspectives, practicing forgiveness, focusing on virtuous action, and implementing mediation and dialogue, students develop invaluable conflict resolution skills. Stoicism provides a framework for students to address conflicts constructively, promoting personal growth, empathy, and virtuous living. By applying Stoic principles to conflict resolution, educators equip students with essential life skills that extend beyond the classroom, preparing them to navigate challenges and cultivate harmonious relationships in their future endeavors. The integration of Stoic techniques for conflict resolution contributes to a peaceful and supportive learning environment, where conflicts are seen as opportunities for growth and mutual understanding.

Teaching Students to Cope with Stress and Anxiety

TEACHING STUDENTS HOW to cope with stress and anxiety is crucial for their overall well-being and academic success. Stoicism offers practical and effective techniques that empower students to manage stressors and develop resilience in the face of challenges. By integrating Stoic principles of acceptance, self-control, and focusing on what is within their power, educators equip students with invaluable tools for navigating stress and anxiety in a healthy and constructive manner.

Emphasize the Stoic Dichotomy of Control

Introduce students to the Stoic dichotomy of control, which distinguishes between what is within their control (their thoughts, actions, and attitudes) and what is not (external events and others' behaviors). Help students understand that they can manage their reactions and attitudes toward stressors, even if they cannot control the events themselves.

The Art of Acceptance

Stoicism encourages acceptance of things beyond our control. Teach students to recognize when they are facing situations they cannot change, and guide them in accepting these circumstances with grace. Encourage them to focus their energy on responding wisely and virtuously to challenges.

Practicing Mindfulness

Introduce mindfulness techniques to help students stay present and focused, reducing stress and anxiety. Mindfulness exercises, such as deep breathing and body scans, can be incorporated into the classroom routine to help students cultivate awareness of their emotions and responses.

Reframing Negative Thoughts

Stoicism emphasizes the power of reframing perspectives. Guide students in identifying and challenging negative thought patterns that contribute to stress and anxiety. Teach them to reframe negative thoughts into more balanced and constructive ones, promoting a healthier outlook on challenges.

Cultivating Resilience

Stoicism teaches that setbacks are opportunities for growth and learning. Encourage students to view challenges as chances to build resilience and strength. Share examples of Stoic figures who faced adversity with courage and determination, inspiring students to adopt a similar mindset.

The Practice of Self-Control

Teach students self-control techniques to manage stress and anxiety. Encourage them to take a moment to pause and reflect before reacting impulsively to stressors. By cultivating self-control, students can respond to challenges with composure and clarity.

Focusing on What is Within Their Power

Remind students to focus on what is within their power during stressful situations. Encourage them to identify actionable steps they can take to address challenges or improve their well-being, even in small ways.

Balancing Work and Rest

Stoicism emphasizes the importance of balance in life. Teach students the value of time management and setting realistic expectations for themselves. Encourage them to prioritize self-care and rest, as well as productive work.

Teaching students to cope with stress and anxiety using Stoic principles empowers them to develop emotional resilience and maintain a healthy perspective on challenges. By emphasizing the dichotomy of control, acceptance, mindfulness, reframing negative thoughts, cultivating resilience, practicing self-control, focusing on what is within their power, and balancing work and rest, educators provide students with practical tools for managing stressors and anxiety in their lives. Stoicism's emphasis on accepting what cannot be changed and focusing on one's inner virtues encourages students to approach stress with composure, wisdom, and self-awareness. By integrating Stoic techniques into their coping strategies, students build valuable life skills that extend beyond the classroom, preparing them to face life's challenges with courage, resilience, and a sense of inner tranquility. Creating a supportive and empowering environment for students to cope with stress aligns with Stoicism's focus on personal growth and the pursuit of virtue for a fulfilling and flourishing life.

Supporting Each Other During Difficult Times

SUPPORTING EACH OTHER during difficult times is a core aspect of cultivating a Stoic-inspired classroom community. Stoicism emphasizes the interconnectedness of all human beings and the importance of collective well-being. By fostering an environment of empathy, compassion, and mutual support, educators create a space where students can navigate challenges together and draw strength from their shared experiences.

Encourage Open Communication

Promote open communication in the classroom, where students feel comfortable sharing their challenges and struggles. Create a safe space for students to express their feelings and thoughts without fear of judgment. By encouraging open communication, students know that they are not alone in facing difficulties and that their classmates and educators are there to support them.

Group Problem-Solving

Facilitate group problem-solving sessions during challenging times. Students can work collaboratively to find solutions and support one another in overcoming obstacles. By engaging in group problem-solving, students learn the value of teamwork, cooperation, and the collective power of their shared efforts.

Peer Support and Buddy Systems

Implement peer support and buddy systems where students are paired up to provide encouragement and assistance during challenging times. This system allows students to lean on each other for emotional support and practical help, reinforcing the idea that they are part of a supportive community.

Compassionate Listening

Teach students the art of compassionate listening, where they actively listen to one another without judgment and with genuine empathy. Encourage students to be present and attentive when their classmates are sharing their struggles, offering a compassionate ear and understanding.

Shared Reflection Circles

Organize shared reflection circles where students can come together to discuss their experiences and challenges. In this supportive environment, students can share insights, strategies for coping, and offer encouragement to one another. These circles reinforce the sense of community and shared responsibility for supporting each other.

Stoic Virtue of Kindness

Emphasize the Stoic virtue of kindness and how it fosters a caring and compassionate community. Encourage students to practice acts of kindness towards one another during difficult times, whether through small gestures or offering a helping hand.

Cultivate a Growth Mindset

Instill a growth mindset in students, teaching them that challenges are opportunities for growth and learning. By embracing challenges with a growth mindset, students view difficult times as stepping stones toward personal development rather than insurmountable obstacles.

Model Supportive Behavior

As educators, model supportive behavior and empathy in your interactions with students. Demonstrate how to offer encouragement, understanding, and kindness during difficult times, setting an example for students to follow.

Supporting each other during difficult times is integral to fostering a Stoic-inspired classroom community. By encouraging open communication, group problem-solving, peer support, compassionate listening, shared reflection circles, and the cultivation of kindness and a growth mindset, educators create a supportive environment where students can lean on one another during challenges. Stoicism's emphasis on interconnectedness and the pursuit of virtue informs this supportive atmosphere, reinforcing the idea that students are part of a caring community that shares in each other's struggles and triumphs. By supporting each other, students develop essential life skills in empathy, compassion, and resilience, enhancing their emotional well-being and academic success. The collaborative effort of supporting each other during difficult times creates a positive and empowering learning environment where students feel valued, understood, and inspired to overcome challenges together.

IX. Empowering Students to Become Leaders

Τοῖς αὑτοῦ μεγάλοις οὐχ ἕτεροι προσκαθίστανται καὶ δούλους ἀδικοῦσι καὶ ἀναξίους, ἐξανίστανται μὲν αὐτῶν, τοὺς δ' αὐτῶν μᾶλλον ἄρχουσιν.

The truly great do not sit in judgment on the lowly or mistreat them, but they outdo them, and especially in conferring benefits. *(Meditations, 7.60)*

Ὅταν δὲ δυσπραγίας ὁ ἄρχων, μὴ ἐπιστρέφειν τὸν βλάπτοντα, ἀλλὰ μᾶλλον αὐτὸν βλάπτειν.

When someone behaves poorly, the leader should not turn against them, but rather correct them. *(Meditations, 9.38)*

Encouraging Student Leadership and Responsibility

EMPOWERING STUDENTS to become leaders is a transformative aspect of cultivating a Stoic-inspired classroom community. Stoicism values the development of virtuous character and the pursuit of excellence, and by encouraging student leadership and responsibility, educators nurture the seeds of leadership potential in each student. Through this process, students learn to embrace challenges, make informed decisions, and take ownership of their actions, fostering personal growth and ethical leadership.

Student-Centered Decision-Making

Involve students in decision-making processes within the classroom. Encourage them to share their ideas and perspectives on various aspects of the learning environment, such as classroom rules, projects, and activities. By actively involving students in decision-making, educators promote a sense of ownership and responsibility for the classroom community.

Leadership Roles and Responsibilities

Assign leadership roles and responsibilities to students. These roles may include classroom monitors, project leaders, or peer mentors. Leadership opportunities provide students with the chance to develop organizational, communication, and problem-solving skills, while also fostering a sense of accountability.

Student-Led Initiatives

Support and encourage student-led initiatives that align with Stoic values and promote positive change within the school or community. Whether it's organizing a charity event or advocating for environmental sustainability, these initiatives empower students to take action and contribute to the common good.

Foster a Growth Mindset

Promote a growth mindset in students, emphasizing that leadership is not fixed but can be developed through effort and perseverance. Encourage students to embrace challenges as opportunities for growth and to view setbacks as learning experiences.

Reflection and Self-Assessment

Encourage students to reflect on their leadership experiences and self-assess their strengths and areas for improvement. Through reflection, students gain insights into their leadership styles and understand how Stoic principles can inform their leadership practices.

Ethical Decision-Making

Teach students the importance of ethical decision-making and the impact their choices can have on others. Guided by Stoic virtues, encourage students to consider the ethical implications of their actions and to prioritize the well-being of the community.

Encourage Supportive Leadership

Promote a leadership style that is supportive and compassionate. Encourage students to lead by example, inspiring others through their actions and fostering a sense of collaboration and camaraderie among peers.

Recognize Leadership Efforts

Recognize and celebrate students' leadership efforts and achievements. Acknowledge the contributions they make to the classroom community and encourage their continued growth as leaders.

Encouraging student leadership and responsibility aligns with Stoicism's emphasis on virtuous character and the pursuit of excellence. By involving students in decision-making, assigning leadership roles and responsibilities, supporting student-led initiatives, fostering a growth mindset, promoting ethical decision-making, encouraging supportive leadership, and recognizing leadership efforts, educators nurture the development of ethical and capable leaders. Empowering students to become leaders not only benefits their personal growth and leadership skills but also contributes to the overall strength and vitality of the classroom community. By embracing Stoic principles in their leadership practices, students learn to lead with integrity, empathy, and a commitment to the common good. The cultivation of student leadership is a transformative aspect of Stoic-inspired education, shaping future leaders who are compassionate, principled, and dedicated to making a positive impact in their communities and beyond.

Instilling the Importance of Ethical Decision-Making

INSTILLING THE IMPORTANCE of ethical decision-making is a fundamental aspect of cultivating Stoicism-inspired leadership in students. Stoicism places great emphasis on living a virtuous life, and ethical decision-making is at the core of virtuous actions. By guiding students to make ethical choices based on Stoic principles, educators equip them with the tools to become principled leaders who prioritize the well-being of others and act with integrity.

Introduce Stoic Ethics

Introduce students to Stoic ethics and the four cardinal virtues: wisdom, courage, justice, and temperance. Explain how these virtues form the foundation of ethical decision-making and how they guide individuals to act in ways that promote the common good.

Analyze Ethical Dilemmas

Present students with ethical dilemmas relevant to their lives and discuss possible courses of action. Encourage students to consider how

Stoic virtues can inform their decisions and how they can choose actions aligned with their principles.

Cultivate Self-Reflection

Teach students the importance of self-reflection when faced with ethical decisions. Encourage them to pause and examine their motivations and potential consequences before making choices. Stoicism emphasizes the need for inner tranquility and self-awareness to act virtuously.

Role Play Ethical Scenarios

Engage students in role-playing activities where they act out ethical scenarios and explore different ways to handle the situations. This exercise allows students to practice ethical decision-making in a safe environment and receive feedback from peers and educators.

Study Stoic Role Models

Study Stoic role models from history and literature who exemplify ethical leadership. Discuss the actions of figures like Marcus Aurelius and Epictetus, and explore how their adherence to Stoic virtues guided their decisions.

Collaborative Ethical Discussions

Encourage collaborative discussions about ethical issues and dilemmas within the classroom community. By engaging in group discussions, students gain different perspectives and learn to empathize with others' viewpoints.

Emphasize Consequences and Impact

Discuss the potential consequences and impact of ethical decisions on individuals and the broader community. Help students understand how their actions affect others and the importance of considering the well-being of all stakeholders in their decision-making.

Celebrate Ethical Leadership

Recognize and celebrate instances of ethical leadership within the classroom. Acknowledge students who demonstrate ethical decision-making and exemplify Stoic virtues in their actions, reinforcing the value of integrity and principled leadership.

Instilling the importance of ethical decision-making in students is a crucial step in cultivating Stoicism-inspired leadership. By introducing Stoic ethics, analyzing ethical dilemmas, cultivating self-reflection, role-playing ethical scenarios, studying Stoic role models, engaging in collaborative discussions, emphasizing consequences and impact, and celebrating ethical leadership, educators guide students to make choices aligned with their principles and values. Ethical decision-making empowers students to become principled leaders who prioritize the well-being of others and act with integrity in various contexts. The integration of ethical decision-making in leadership aligns with Stoicism's emphasis on virtuous character and the pursuit of the common good. As students internalize the importance of ethical decision-making, they develop the capacity to lead with wisdom, courage, justice, and temperance, making a positive impact on their communities and embodying the core values of Stoicism.

Inspiring Students to be Role Models for Others

INSPIRING STUDENTS to be role models for others is a transformative aspect of cultivating Stoicism-inspired leadership in the classroom. Stoicism places great importance on living a life of virtue and setting an example for others to follow. By fostering a culture of positive influence and ethical leadership, educators empower students to embrace their roles as leaders and inspire their peers to act with wisdom, courage, justice, and temperance.

Teach the Power of Influence

Educate students about the power of influence and the impact their actions can have on others. Help them recognize that they possess the ability to influence their peers positively through their words, actions, and choices.

Share Stories of Ethical Leadership

Share stories of individuals who exemplify ethical leadership and have made a positive impact on their communities. These stories can come from history, literature, or contemporary role models. Discuss how these individuals' adherence to Stoic principles inspired others to follow their lead.

Cultivate Stoic Virtues

Guide students in cultivating Stoic virtues within themselves, such as wisdom, courage, justice, and temperance. Encourage them to integrate these virtues into their daily lives and interactions with others, becoming beacons of virtue and ethical conduct.

Encourage Acts of Kindness and Empathy

Promote acts of kindness, empathy, and compassion within the classroom community. Encourage students to be mindful of each other's feelings and needs, fostering an environment of mutual support and understanding.

Emphasize the Ripple Effect

Highlight the ripple effect of positive leadership and ethical behavior. Discuss how one student's virtuous actions can inspire others to follow suit, creating a chain reaction of positive influence throughout the classroom and beyond.

Recognize and Celebrate Virtuous Behavior

Recognize and celebrate instances of virtuous behavior and ethical leadership among students. Acknowledge and praise students who exemplify Stoic virtues and serve as role models for their peers.

Encourage Peer Mentorship

Promote peer mentorship within the classroom, where students support and guide one another in their personal growth and leadership journey. Peer mentorship reinforces the concept of students inspiring and motivating each other to be their best selves.

Foster a Supportive Community

Create a supportive classroom community where students feel comfortable sharing their values and aspirations openly. In this environment, students are more likely to support and encourage one another's growth as ethical leaders.

Inspiring students to be role models for others is an essential aspect of cultivating Stoicism-inspired leadership in the classroom. By teaching the power of influence, sharing stories of ethical leadership, cultivating Stoic virtues, encouraging acts of kindness and empathy, emphasizing the ripple effect, recognizing and celebrating virtuous behavior, promoting peer mentorship, and fostering a supportive community, educators empower students to embrace their roles as ethical leaders and inspire their peers through their words and actions. Stoicism's emphasis on virtuous living and the pursuit of excellence aligns with the notion of inspiring others to follow a path of wisdom, courage, justice, and temperance. As students embrace their roles as positive role models, they contribute to a flourishing and harmonious learning environment where ethical leadership becomes a guiding principle for all. The inspiration students provide to their peers has a profound impact on the classroom community, reinforcing the values of integrity, compassion, and the pursuit of the common good. By inspiring students to be role models for others, educators cultivate a culture of ethical leadership that extends beyond the classroom, enriching the lives of all those touched by their virtuous influence.

X. Sustaining the Stoic Classroom Community

Ἀλλὰ ἀκριβῶς μελέτω τοῦτο, εἰ πού τις αὐτῶν ἔλαβεν.

But let us be precise about it: if anyone got hold of them [our beliefs], he would find us standing firm. (Enchiridion, 30)

Ἔκκεισο δὲ τοῦτο μόνον, εἰ πολλάκις τοῦτο ἐπὶ σὲ παραγίγνεται, τὸ μὴ δεῖν ἐν τῇ πολλοῦ κατάλυσιν οὐδὲν τοιοῦτον ὑπολείπεσθαι.

And the only thing of real value is to not let their abuse [negative opinions] leave its mark on you, to remain calm and kind. (Meditations, 12.36)

Continuous Reinforcement of Stoic Values

SUSTAINING THE STOIC classroom community requires continuous reinforcement of Stoic values throughout the learning journey. Stoicism emphasizes the cultivation of virtuous character and the pursuit of wisdom, courage, justice, and temperance. By integrating Stoic values into the fabric of the classroom community, educators create an environment that fosters personal growth, ethical decision-making, and compassionate interactions.

Consistent Language and Messaging

Use consistent language and messaging that reflects Stoic values in classroom discussions, guidelines, and activities. Regularly remind students of the importance of virtues such as wisdom, courage, justice, and temperance in their academic and personal lives.

Daily Stoic Reflections

Incorporate daily Stoic reflections as part of the classroom routine. Encourage students to take a few moments each day for introspection and self-awareness, considering how they can embody Stoic virtues in their actions and responses to challenges.

Stoic Quotes and Literature

Introduce Stoic quotes and excerpts from Stoic literature as a source of inspiration and guidance. Share passages that highlight the importance of ethical conduct, resilience, and personal growth, allowing students to reflect on their relevance to their lives.

Reinforce Virtuous Behavior

Recognize and reinforce virtuous behavior among students. Celebrate instances where students demonstrate Stoic values through acts of kindness, compassion, and leadership, fostering a culture that values and encourages ethical conduct.

Classroom Pledge or Creed

Create a classroom pledge or creed based on Stoic principles. Involve students in crafting the pledge, and encourage them to commit to living by these principles in their interactions with peers and within the learning environment.

Stoic-Themed Projects

Incorporate Stoic-themed projects and activities that allow students to explore and apply Stoic values in real-life scenarios. These projects provide opportunities for students to delve deeper into Stoicism and its practical implications.

Stoic Role Models

Introduce students to Stoic role models from history and contemporary life. Explore how these figures embodied Stoic values and left a positive impact on the world. Discuss how students can draw inspiration from these role models in their own lives.

Cultivate a Growth Mindset

Cultivate a growth mindset within the classroom community. Encourage students to see challenges as opportunities for growth and learning, aligning with Stoic principles that view adversity as a chance to develop resilience and wisdom.

Continuous reinforcement of Stoic values sustains the Stoic classroom community by creating an environment that nurtures virtuous character and ethical leadership. Through consistent language and messaging, daily Stoic reflections, the use of Stoic quotes and literature, reinforcing virtuous behavior, creating a classroom pledge or creed, incorporating Stoic-themed projects, introducing Stoic role models, and cultivating a growth mindset, educators create a culture that embodies Stoic ideals. By integrating Stoic values into various aspects of the classroom experience, students learn to navigate challenges with wisdom, courage, justice, and temperance, fostering personal growth and compassionate interactions with their peers. The continuous reinforcement of Stoic values instills a sense of purpose and shared responsibility within the classroom community, guiding students towards a life of virtue and ethical leadership. As students internalize Stoic principles and apply them to their daily lives, they contribute to a thriving and harmonious learning environment that exemplifies the core values of Stoicism.

Celebrating Progress and Growth in Students

CELEBRATING PROGRESS and growth in students is a crucial aspect of sustaining the Stoic classroom community. Stoicism emphasizes personal development and the pursuit of virtue, and by recognizing and celebrating students' progress, educators reinforce the importance of continuous improvement and self-awareness. Celebratory moments not only foster a positive and encouraging learning environment but also inspire students to persevere in their pursuit of wisdom, courage, justice, and temperance.

Acknowledge Efforts and Improvements

Acknowledge students' efforts and improvements, regardless of the outcomes. Celebrate the journey of growth and the commitment to learning and developing virtuous character.

Share Growth Stories

Share growth stories and examples of students who have overcome challenges and demonstrated Stoic values in their actions. These stories serve as inspirations for others and demonstrate the power of perseverance and virtue.

Growth-Oriented Feedback

Provide growth-oriented feedback that focuses on students' progress and areas for improvement. Encourage students to view feedback as an opportunity for learning and refinement, aligning with Stoic principles of self-awareness and self-improvement.

Stoic Progress Journals

Introduce Stoic progress journals where students can document their reflections on personal growth and instances where they demonstrated Stoic values. These journals serve as a record of their journey and provide a means for self-assessment.

Stoic Achievement Awards

Create Stoic achievement awards to recognize students who exemplify Stoic virtues in their actions and interactions. These awards can highlight courage, wisdom, justice, temperance, and other virtuous behaviors.

Celebrate Acts of Kindness

Celebrate acts of kindness and compassion demonstrated by students within the classroom community. Recognize the positive impact these actions have on the overall classroom culture.

Growth Showcases

Host growth showcases or presentations where students share their personal growth stories and reflections. These showcases provide a platform for students to celebrate their progress and inspire their peers.

Peer Recognition

Encourage peer recognition within the classroom community. Allow students to acknowledge and appreciate each other's growth and virtuous behavior, fostering a culture of support and encouragement.

Celebrating progress and growth in students sustains the Stoic classroom community by reinforcing the importance of continuous improvement and the pursuit of virtue. Through acknowledging efforts and improvements, sharing growth stories, providing growth-oriented feedback, introducing Stoic progress journals, creating Stoic achievement awards, celebrating acts of kindness, hosting growth showcases, and encouraging peer recognition, educators create a culture of celebration and encouragement. Celebratory moments inspire students to embrace challenges and persevere in their journey to embody Stoic virtues. By recognizing and celebrating the progress of each student, educators demonstrate the value they place on personal development and ethical conduct. This fosters a positive and empowering learning environment where students feel supported and motivated to pursue wisdom, courage, justice, and temperance in their lives. As students celebrate their growth and virtuous actions, they contribute to a flourishing Stoic classroom community, where the pursuit of excellence and ethical leadership is celebrated and cherished.

Creating a Legacy of Empathy and Resilience for Future Generations

CREATING A LEGACY OF empathy and resilience for future generations is a profound and enduring aspect of sustaining the Stoic classroom community. Stoicism teaches the interconnectedness of humanity and the importance of leaving a positive impact on others. By fostering empathy and resilience in students, educators empower them to become compassionate and principled leaders who, in turn, inspire future generations to embody Stoic virtues.

Cultivate Empathy Through Understanding

Cultivate empathy through understanding the experiences and perspectives of others. Encourage students to put themselves in the shoes of their peers and to consider the emotions and challenges they might be facing. By nurturing empathy, students learn to connect with others on a deeper level and cultivate compassion.

Encourage Acts of Kindness and Service

Encourage acts of kindness and service within the classroom community and beyond. Empower students to actively look for opportunities to support and uplift others, fostering a culture of empathy and benevolence.

Model Resilience in Adversity

As educators, model resilience in the face of adversity and challenges. Demonstrating how to approach setbacks with courage and wisdom inspires students to develop their own resilience and persevere through difficult times.

Discuss Stoic Role Models of Resilience

Discuss Stoic role models who have demonstrated remarkable resilience in their lives. Explore the stories of historical figures or contemporary individuals who overcame obstacles with Stoic virtues. These examples serve as inspirations for students to develop their own resilience.

Reflect on the Ripple Effect

Encourage students to reflect on the ripple effect of their actions on others and future generations. Help them understand the significance of their choices and the potential long-term impact of their virtuous behavior.

Integrate Stoic Virtues in Classroom Culture

Integrate Stoic virtues, such as courage, justice, and temperance, into the classroom culture and community. By practicing these virtues daily, students internalize them and carry them forward into their lives beyond the classroom.

Discuss the Importance of Leaving a Positive Legacy

Discuss the concept of leaving a positive legacy and the responsibility each individual has in shaping the world for future generations. Stoicism emphasizes the importance of living a life of virtue and contributing to the greater good.

Engage in Community Service Projects

Engage in community service projects that align with Stoic values, promoting empathy and resilience. Students can participate in initiatives that support vulnerable communities, reinforcing the importance of serving others.

Creating a legacy of empathy and resilience for future generations is a powerful and transformative aspect of sustaining the Stoic classroom community. By cultivating empathy through understanding, encouraging acts of kindness and service, modeling resilience in adversity, discussing Stoic role models of resilience, reflecting on the ripple effect of actions, integrating Stoic virtues in the classroom culture, discussing the importance of leaving a positive legacy, and engaging in community service projects, educators empower students to become compassionate and resilient leaders. The cultivation of empathy and resilience aligns with Stoicism's emphasis on virtuous character and the interconnectedness of humanity. As students develop empathy and resilience, they embody Stoic values and contribute to a positive and compassionate classroom community. Moreover, these virtues become part of the students' lifelong toolkit, inspiring them to create a legacy of empathy and resilience that will shape the world for future generations. By nurturing a generation of compassionate and principled leaders, the Stoic classroom community leaves an enduring and positive impact on society, fostering a legacy of empathy and resilience that transcends time and continues to inspire and uplift future generations.

XI. Conclusion

—

Κόσμῳ προσέχειν καὶ τοῖς ἄστροις, δρόμον τε σῶν ὁρᾶν, ταῖς συμπαρούσαις ὁρμᾶσθαι.

Dwell on the beauty of life. Watch the stars, and see yourself running with them. *(Meditations, 7.47)*

Ὁδός μελετῆς, λόγος.

The path to tranquility, reason. *(Meditations, 6.30)*

Recap of the Benefits of a Stoic-Inspired Classroom Community

THE JOURNEY OF CULTIVATING a Stoic-inspired classroom community comes with numerous benefits that enrich the lives of students and educators alike. Let's recap the key advantages of fostering a Stoic-influenced learning environment:

- **Enhanced Classroom Dynamics:** By embracing Stoic values such as empathy, compassion, and resilience, the classroom community becomes more cohesive and supportive. Students feel valued and understood, fostering a positive and empowering learning environment.
- **Ethical Leadership:** Instilling the importance of ethical decision-making and encouraging student leadership empowers students to become principled leaders. They learn to prioritize the well-being of others and act with integrity, fostering a culture of ethical leadership within the classroom.
- **Resilience and Growth Mindset:** Through Stoic teachings, students learn to embrace challenges as opportunities for growth. They develop a growth mindset and learn to approach

setbacks with courage and wisdom, leading to enhanced resilience and perseverance.

- **Positive Interactions:** By promoting kindness, cooperation, and respect, the classroom community becomes a space where positive interactions flourish. Students develop strong interpersonal skills and build meaningful connections with their peers.

- **Mindfulness and Self-Reflection:** Integrating mindfulness practices and self-reflection exercises nurtures students' self-awareness and emotional intelligence. They learn to manage their emotions and responses effectively, enhancing their overall well-being.

- **Empathy and Compassion:** Fostering empathy as a key virtue in Stoicism creates a culture of understanding and support. Students learn to empathize with others and develop compassion, leading to a more empathetic and caring community.

- **Legacy of Virtuous Influence:** Sustaining a Stoic classroom community creates a legacy of virtue and ethical conduct. As students embody Stoic principles and become role models for others, they inspire future generations to pursue wisdom, justice, courage, and temperance.

- **Academic and Personal Growth:** The Stoic-inspired classroom community promotes academic excellence and personal growth. Students are encouraged to embrace challenges, take responsibility for their learning, and strive for continuous improvement.

- **Positive Impact on Society:** By instilling Stoic virtues and values, educators nurture a generation of compassionate and principled leaders who can positively impact society. These students become agents of positive change, contributing to a more harmonious and empathetic world.

- **Lifelong Skills and Mindset:** The Stoic-inspired classroom community equips students with lifelong skills and a mindset that extends far beyond the classroom. They carry these virtues and principles into their future endeavors, making a meaningful impact in various aspects of their lives.

A Stoic-inspired classroom community is a transformative space where students cultivate virtues, embrace challenges, and develop ethical leadership. The benefits of such an environment are vast and encompass enhanced classroom dynamics, ethical leadership, resilience, positive interactions, mindfulness, empathy, and a lasting legacy of virtuous influence. The Stoic principles and values foster academic and personal growth, preparing students to be compassionate, principled, and resilient individuals who positively impact society. By nurturing a Stoic-inspired classroom community, educators create a learning environment that fosters personal development, empathy, and a commitment to virtuous living. As students carry these principles into their lives beyond the classroom, they become beacons of compassion and ethical leadership, creating a ripple effect of positive change in the world. The journey of cultivating a Stoic-inspired classroom community is an investment in the future, where the impact of ethical conduct and virtuous living extends far beyond the boundaries of the classroom, shaping a brighter and more empathetic future for generations to come.

Final Thoughts on Building a Positive and Enduring Learning Environment

BUILDING A POSITIVE and enduring learning environment through Stoicism is a transformative and empowering journey for educators and students alike. As we reflect on the principles and practices discussed throughout this book, let us delve into the final thoughts on how to create a lasting and enriching classroom community:

- **Embrace Stoic Principles:** Embody Stoic principles such as wisdom, courage, justice, and temperance as an educator. By modeling these virtues, you inspire students to follow suit and create a classroom culture based on ethical conduct and compassionate interactions.

- **Foster a Sense of Belonging:** Cultivate a sense of belonging within the classroom community. Encourage open communication, active listening, and collaboration, allowing each student to feel valued and respected.

- **Cultivate Self-Awareness:** Integrate mindfulness practices and self-reflection exercises to nurture students' self-awareness. Help them develop emotional intelligence and become more attuned to their thoughts, feelings, and behaviors.

- **Encourage Ethical Decision-Making:** Instill the importance of ethical decision-making and the impact of choices on others. Teach students to consider the well-being of all stakeholders and act with integrity.
- **Celebrate Growth and Resilience:** Recognize and celebrate students' progress and resilience. Create a culture where effort, improvement, and perseverance are acknowledged and encouraged.
- **Inspire Empathy and Compassion:** Foster empathy as a key virtue in Stoicism and encourage acts of kindness and service. Cultivate a culture of empathy and compassion where students support and uplift one another.
- **Empower Student Leadership:** Empower students to become ethical leaders by involving them in decision-making and assigning leadership roles. Encourage them to lead with integrity and inspire others through their actions.
- **Cultivate a Growth Mindset:** Promote a growth mindset where challenges are viewed as opportunities for growth and learning. Encourage students to embrace setbacks as stepping stones to success.
- **Reflect on the Ripple Effect:** Help students understand the impact of their actions on others and society. Inspire them to leave a positive legacy by living a life of virtue and compassion.
- **Create Lifelong Learners:** Instill a love for learning and a desire for continuous improvement in students. Encourage them to be curious, open-minded, and engaged in their pursuit of knowledge.

Building a positive and enduring learning environment through Stoicism is a transformative journey that requires dedication, compassion, and principled leadership. By embracing Stoic principles, fostering a sense of belonging, cultivating self-awareness, encouraging ethical decision-making, celebrating growth and resilience, inspiring empathy and compassion, empowering student leadership, promoting a growth mindset, reflecting on the ripple effect of actions, and creating lifelong learners, educators create a classroom community that nurtures personal and academic growth.

As educators, you have the power to shape not only students' academic achievements but also their character and values. By integrating Stoicism into the classroom, you create a space where ethical conduct, empathy, and resilience are celebrated and cherished. The impact of building such a learning environment extends far beyond the confines of the classroom, leaving a positive and lasting influence on students' lives and the world they inhabit.

Embrace the principles of Stoicism and guide your students on a journey of personal growth and ethical leadership. By fostering a positive and enduring learning environment, you sow the seeds of compassion, resilience, and wisdom, creating a legacy that will inspire future generations to come. As you embark on this transformative path, remember that the journey of cultivating a Stoic-inspired classroom community is a profound investment in the future, shaping compassionate and principled individuals who will make a positive impact on society and embody the core values of Stoicism throughout their lives.

Encouragement for Educators to Embrace Stoic Values in their Teaching Practices

AS EDUCATORS, EMBRACING Stoic values in your teaching practices can have a profound and transformative impact on your classroom community and the lives of your students. Let's delve into the encouragement to incorporate Stoicism into your teaching approach:

- **Lead by Example:** Embrace Stoic principles and virtues in your own life and actions. By modeling wisdom, courage, justice, and temperance, you inspire your students to embody these values in their own lives.

- **Nurture Compassionate Interactions:** Foster a culture of empathy and compassion within the classroom. Encourage students to support and uplift one another, creating an environment where kindness and understanding thrive.

- **Encourage Growth and Resilience:** Cultivate a growth mindset in your teaching practices. Emphasize the importance of embracing challenges as opportunities for growth and teach students to persevere through setbacks with courage and resilience.

- **Integrate Stoic Philosophy:** Integrate Stoic philosophy into your lesson plans and discussions. Use Stoic quotes, stories, and concepts to inspire and guide students in their personal and academic growth.

- **Promote Ethical Decision-Making:** Instill the importance of ethical decision-making and integrity. Encourage students to consider the consequences of their actions and prioritize the well-being of others.

- **Foster Inclusivity and Belonging:** Create an inclusive and welcoming classroom environment where every student feels valued and respected. Encourage open dialogue and active listening, fostering a sense of belonging for all.

- **Empower Student Leadership:** Empower students to take on leadership roles and make meaningful contributions to the classroom community. Encourage them to lead with integrity and compassion.

- **Reflect on Growth and Progress:** Celebrate students' growth and progress, regardless of their starting point. Acknowledge effort, improvement, and resilience, inspiring students to continue striving for excellence.

- **Practice Mindfulness:** Integrate mindfulness practices into the classroom routine. Teach students to be present in the moment and develop self-awareness, enhancing their emotional intelligence.

- **Foster a Love for Learning:** Cultivate a love for learning and a curiosity-driven mindset. Encourage students to explore new ideas and concepts, fostering a lifelong passion for knowledge.

Embracing Stoic values in your teaching practices is an invitation to transform your classroom community into a space of compassion, ethical conduct, and personal growth. By leading by example, nurturing compassionate interactions, encouraging growth and resilience, integrating Stoic philosophy, promoting ethical decision-making, fostering inclusivity and belonging, empowering student leadership, reflecting on growth and progress, practicing mindfulness, and fostering a love for learning, you create a learning environment that cultivates virtuous character and principled leadership.

As an educator, you have the unique opportunity to shape not only students' academic achievements but also their values and character. Embracing Stoic values in your teaching practices allows you to empower your students to become compassionate, resilient, and ethical leaders who positively impact the world. The journey of incorporating Stoicism into your teaching approach is a transformative one that extends far beyond the classroom, leaving a lasting legacy of compassion, wisdom, and principled living. By embracing Stoic values in your teaching practices, you contribute to a brighter and more empathetic future, inspiring future generations to embrace ethical leadership and embody the core values of Stoicism.

Further Reading

AURELIUS, M. (2021). *Meditations*. United States: Dover Publications.

Epictetus. (2015). *The Enchiridion*. United States: Lulu.com.

Holiday, R., Hanselman, S. (2016). *The Daily Stoic: 366 Meditations on Wisdom, Perseverance, and the Art of Living*. United Kingdom: Penguin Publishing Group.

Seneca, L. A. (2015). *Letters on Ethics: To Lucilius*. United Kingdom: University of Chicago Press.

Don't miss out!

Visit the website below and you can sign up to receive emails whenever Cheryl Angst publishes a new book. There's no charge and no obligation.

https://books2read.com/r/B-A-SBAY-ZDAMC

BOOKS 2 READ

Connecting independent readers to independent writers.

About the Author

Cheryl Angst has been teaching in the classroom for over twenty-five years. With a Masters in curriculum and instruction, her passion centers around finding tips, tricks, and strategies to enhance her practice.

Cheryl is a firm believer that learning should be fun for both the students and the teacher. If it isn't engaging, or doesn't spark joy, it's likely able to be done differently.

The "Quick Reads for Busy Educators" series is designed to maximize the precious time educators have. Each book is short enough to be read in an hour or less, but contains a wealth of information on the topic. Some books are overviews of strategies and approaches (enough to help educators decide if it's for them) and some are deeper dives into specific aspects of those larger approaches. This allows busy educators to grab the information they need quickly and efficiently.

If there's a topic you'd like to see covered in the "Quick Reads" series, please let us know!